PARENTING STYLES IN INDIA

By the same author

1. The Development of Personality in the Indian Ecology
2. Indian Adolescents in the Modernising World
3. The Power of Politics in the Govt. of the Poor in India

About the Author

Dr. Margaret Khalakdina is an independent consultant in the field of Human Development. She completed her Masters and Doctorate at Syracuse and Cornell Universities respectively. She has been: *Executive Director, Indian Council for Child Welfare; Dean, College of Home Science, Haryana Agricultural University, Hissar; Advisor to Vice-Chancellor, Himachal Pradesh Agricultural University, Palampur.* She has also taught at Nirmala Niketan College, Mumbai and SNDT College of Home Science, Mumbai.

She has been a Consultant to WHO and FAO in Egypt and Uganda and has also worked for UNICEF in African countries of Ethiopia and Somalia.

Dr. Khalakdina has authored and published a number of books on Early Child Care and Human Development in India, such as *Early Child Care in India* (1997); *Human Development in the Indian Context: A Socio-cultural Focus* (two volumes, 2009 and 2011); *The Development of Personality in the Indian Ecology* (2012), *The Power of Politics in the Governance of the Poor in India* (2013) and *Indian Adolescents in the Modernising World* (2015). She has authored several articles and papers published in various journals on early childcare, human development and human ecology.

PARENTING STYLES IN INDIA

Margaret Khalakdina

CONCEPT PUBLISHING COMPANY PVT. LTD.
NEW DELHI-110059

ISBN-13: 978-93-5125-286-3 (HB)

First Published 2017

Published and Printed by

Concept
Since 1974

Concept Publishing Company Pvt. Ltd.
Regd. Office:
A/15-16, Commercial Block, Mohan Garden,
New Delhi-110059 (INDIA)
Phones : 25351460, 25351794, *Fax* : 091-11-25357109
Email : publishing@conceptpub.com
Website: www.conceptpub.com

Cataloging in Publication Data—DK Courtesy: D.K. Agencies (P) Ltd. <docinfo@dkagencies.com>

Khalakdina, Margaret, author.
Parenting styles in India / Margaret Khalakdina.
pages cm
Includes bibliographical references and index.
ISBN 9789351252559 (PB)
ISBN 9789351252863 (HB)

1. Parenting—India. I. Title.

HQ755.8.K43 2017 DDC 649.1 23

Foreword
Styles and Standards in Parenting: Bringing Theory to Culture

At the outset, I must declare how humbled I am with the task of writing this piece. Margaret Khalakdina has been my teacher and mentor. Hence, this invitation resulted in an initial panic. How does one introduce a work by someone from whom one has learned so much? I do hope to do justice to this book where the author negotiates the wide-ranging terrain of Indian culture and family life to bring it within the discussion of parenting styles and personality development. It is a task that sometimes leaves reality bulging out at the seams of theoretical straightjacketing. This much we do know, the early interactions between adults and children influences who they become, although the details are often fuzzy.

The Secret of Childhood

Childhood is as an inscrutable phase of life whose mysteries will never been fully known, primarily on account of childhood amnesia. Whatever we remember from our early years is profoundly mediated by what we hear about ourselves. The extended altiriciality[1] of the human infant makes for protracted periods of contact and dependence on adults in comparison with other animals. Thus, the early interactions with adults and older children make a lasting impression on the growing

1. Needing care and nourishment.

child. Yet, the child is also an active being and can, in fact, greatly alter family life once it arrives. Meanwhile, the journey to discover the secret worlds of children is now a well-established field.

We see evidence of protective parents instinctively caring for the young among higher animals, but with *Homo sapiens*, nurture takes on a whole new meaning. The propensity for culture and communication has added much complexity to the task of raising the offspring to maturity. We are able to instruct, plan and imagine the future of our families, thereby altering the experiences of the present. Temporality is key to human developmental processes, not only because the past influences the future, but also because the imagined future deeply influences what we do today (Abbey, 2015; Valsiner, 2007). Among the technologically advanced, 'parenting' has become a contentious issue in today's world. Parents and family members concerned with the child's well-being spend much of their time, energy and resources towards structuring children's lives for a 'better' future. Thus, parenting as an activity has lost its innocence, children do not merely grow-up any more, they are 'brought-up'.

Between Universal Standards and Cultural Diversity

Today's parents thus straddle the precarious space between global trends and cultural themes in parenting. On the one hand we have the UNCRC[2] guidelines on childhood and children's rights and, on the other, we have endless diversity. Several countries have established services for the protection of children. But, in many countries there is increasing evidence of a lower tolerance of parenting practices of immigrant parents who come from culturally different backgrounds. Several such cases have been reported about Indian families residing in other countries where sleeping together with parents, feeding the child by hand and physical punishment are seen as "abusive". At the same time,

2. https://www.unicef.org/crc/

anthropological evidence displays fascinating variations in the care-settings and routines that we are increasingly becoming aware of. Babies are swaddled, strapped, spanked and supported with a mind-blowing variety of ways. India itself has a rich variation of folk practices related to the care of children, as the author reports in this book.

One could invoke Bauman's expression 'liquid modernity' (Bauman, 2012) to illustrate the fragility and uncertainty of modern lives that leaves many parents with doubts and fears about raising their children. Bauman argues that the weight and depth of tradition have been replaced by fluidity and uncertainty in all dimensions of our lives. The relative weakening of traditional beliefs and the confrontation with popular science and global trends in demography and family life has caused some anxiety among people who are then forced to think about how they are bringing up their children. Many chose to delay and deny having children, which has led to negative population growth in some countries, an unimaginable outcome in the past, where children were seen as an inevitable outcome of adult life. Although the awareness that early experiences impact an emerging individual are sprinkled in many cultural sources like myths and stories, the consolidation of a theory is owed to Freud's theory of psychoanalysis. This has been followed by several important theories, one of which has been selected as the template for this book, the theory of Parenting Styles, first postulated by Baumrind (1966).

Parents and family members work towards what they believe to be the best for their children deciding when to intervene and when to let go, further compounded by the contingent responses of individual children, the key elements being the demand placed on the child and the responsiveness to the child by the interacting adult. These are habitual and consistent and have long-term impact on children's developing personality, Baumrind argues. These choices are made with intimate knowledge of the resources, both physical and social, thereby creating the 'place' within which a child develops.

The present book provides its audience with several perspectives on issues relating to parenting, using the theory of parenting styles as a guiding principle. While addressing the large diversity in ecology and culture within the Indian subcontinent, Khalakdina artfully navigates the scene between the depth of ancient knowledge and the diversity of contemporary lives. Instructive both regarding cultural diversity and scientific research, the author brings together a wide-ranging discussion about the fact that underlying manifested practices in the care of children, there are discernible patterns that can be classified as specific styles in parenting. This refers primarily to the tendency to restrict, discuss or ignore children's behaviour habitually. Some important clues are provided on how a theory based on the ideology of a nuclear family setting may play out in fundamentally different cultural spaces, that of multiple caregiving, for instance. This is where the author pushes for more research. As Khalakdina suggests at the outset, this book is intended as an impetus to Indian scholars to find aspects of family life to explore through research targeted at culturally specific patterns of child-rearing. This book is an important addition to the library resources on Indian childhood and family life, and a personal honour for me to write for.

Mumbai **Nandita Chaudhary**
January 2017

References

Abbey, E. (2015). Temporality and the boundary between the present and future. In In, L.M. Simão, D. S. Guimarães and J. Valsiner (Eds.), *Temporality: Culture in the Flow of Human Experience* (pp. 333-352). Charlotte, NC: Information Age.

Bauman, Z. (2012). *Liquid Modernity*. Cambridge: UK Polity Press.

Baumrind, D. (1966). Effects of Authoritative Parental Control on Child Behaviour, *Child Development, 37(4)*: 887-907.

Valsiner, J. (2007). *Culture in Minds and Societies: Foundations of a Cultural Psychology*. New Delhi: Sage.

Preface

This document deals with the generalized theme of parenting styles in India. It emphasizes the possibilities of relationships between the nurturer, namely the parent, and the nurtured, namely the child. There are specific references to the Indian situation as we know the themes that exist currently about these relationships. No doubt the kaleidoscope of interactions between the parent and the progeny will change to some degree from decade to decade and have been so over the centuries. What one can say now with certainty about parent-child interaction may change in some places over time and space, depending upon the race, the ethnicity, the region, the religion and the socio-psychological norms existent at one time and one period. However, as technology and sophisticated information increases, it will add changes to the paradigm of interaction between the nurturer and the nurtured. This book will also deal with the ecological, the socio-psychological and additive factors which will influence the parent-child interactional activities. There are, however, certain socio-psychological conceptualizations which are general as well as specific. The general types spring from the phylogeny of the human being, while the ontogeny is related to the variations created by differences in population and sub-population characteristics in the different thematic behaviours of parent and child. As one writes this book, perhaps there are others in the making describing different behaviours in parent-child interactions in different ecologies, economies, demographies and other extraneous factors. If one were to turn over the leaves of time, parent-child interactions will be differentiated according to the variables affecting the particular group of people living in different areas, in different climes and varied experiences in economy, psychology and sociology.

The specific references are with whatever material is informative for understanding the parent-child interaction processes. In India, while it is an age-old culture, lifestyles are gradually changing. There is much to know from the Mohenjo-Daro and Harappa times of history and from the ongoing twenty first century. There is little doubt that by the twenty second century, there will be expected changes in the lifestyles, the laws, the legalities, the social realities and the economies of different countries, and yet again within each country, differences in styles of living will occur. Similar differences will be found in the Indian culture and its sub-cultures.

It is quite possible that in the next century human beings might visit Mars and find a totally different environment and its inhabitants. But, so far as is known, the human mind during this age and stage develops on the existent material—spoken, written, communicated—that exists between and among the developed and developing countries. Also, the occurance of their expansion, their interests as nations and the politics that generate these differentiation affecting human interaction in the population and sub-population of India. However, the thematic value of interaction continues to be increasing in terms of the development of relationships as the individual grows chronologically. In point of that the writing of this book gives rise to many hypotheses which need to be developed and researched in order to add greater information on parent and child relationships in particular cultures, such as India.

Differentiation also occurs on the basis of differences between the developed and developing countries. Among the developing countries, in India's development is very fast, ecologically, technologically and in socio-psychological aspects in comparison to other developing countries and more, clearly, in relationship to the developed world. It is, therefore, essential in this book to stress the differences where they are observable and give rise to much more proactive hypothetical information which, therefore, needs to be tested.

The southern-most tip of the African continent has not only the original Africans, but also those who have transmigrated from Europe like the Germans to South Africa, the English to Australia and even in the various countries in South America. The two large democracies which tend to remain constant are the USA and India and, therefore, it is essential that whatever development that takes place is to be documented and included in the expansion of understanding the psyche of the various regions and, in this book, that of the Indian. It is expected that the reading of this book will challenge the minds of the thinking educated people in the world to expand and analyze further information on the adult-child interaction processes that exists in India at current times. Over the decades, India has moved its focus from depending upon traditional ways of living to include also modern ways with the incoming of European people, and the interaction with the global world and the nexus it is forming with the worlds of the far-east. During such continuous paradigm of interaction with other countries, the Indian people transit from one status of education to another. From the points of view of phylogeny and ontogeny, these parameters will change over time and space. These two paradigms interact and give rise to understanding of the Indian people and adult-child interaction processes that affect the development of the child which influence adult and child interactions.

Each one of the nationalities in the world differs in their main ethnographic profiles and yet much more needs to be known about these various countries and much more so of India, to gain a better perspective on the adult-child interaction in the developing world, such as India. Hence, this book attempts to provide as much information as is currently available to understand the way parents bring-up their children and their different styles of interaction.

The information in this book stimulates and stirs the thinking mind to develop and research on the various aspects that will cue the mind to develop the hypotheses which could arise from the contents of this book.

Acknowledgements

I express my sincere gratitude and thanks to Mr. M. K. Shaji and Mrs. Shakuntala Dixit for their sincere assistance and cooperation in writing this book. I also express my sincere gratitudes to my children Rolando, Asheena, Arshad and Magda who have all along been supportive in my writing endeavours. I am also grateful to several of my friends, colleagues and former students who have given me their time. A special thanks to Ms. Nandita Chaudhary for writing the Foreword to this book.

New Delhi **M. Khalakdina**

Contents

1
Introduction

In the modernizing world of today, there is greater research available on the social psychological and economic aspects involved in the upbringing of the new generation, not only in general terms but also as applicable to specific cultural contexts. Generally, there is a great emphasis on parent-child relationships and their interactions. Parent-child relationships in India has to take into account the fact that in India there is a bewildering array of human ecologies in heterogeneous areas and sub-cultures. Not only are there ecological differences like the urban, semi-urban, rural interior villages, but also several tribal areas. These different ecological areas and sub-cultures in India indicate the different approaches the parents use in their interaction with their progeny. This document looks into the various kinds of parenting styles followed by the average Indian parent in the varying ecologies that make up the totality of the Indian generic situations that give rise to such differences in the nurturing processes.

Parental ideologies about nurturant practices have undergone change over a period of time. Modern parenting practices are mixed with various aspects brought over from the traditional styles used in the past. Most parents use a variety of parenting styles depending upon their culture, societal demands, their own personalities, and the economic and geo-ecological situations in which they live. The patterns of parenting styles and their impact on the development of the child are amplified in this document. It is essential to understand the characteristics of the interactions between the parent and the child as they act and react upon the cues transmitting between them and as they are influenced by the extraneous variables in the environment. It is also to be understood what are the specific socio-cultural factors influencing the parenting styles such as the ethnicity, caste, religion and demographic factors. The different socio-economic environments influence the interactions between the nurturant and nurtured, giving rise to differential perspectives and perceptions regarding parenting styles. The socio-economic class is an important influencing variable in the interaction between the parent and the child.

The impact of social changes on childhood in India deserves attention. Parenting styles change according to the changes taking place in a particular society and sub-society. Such changes include, for example, educational and technological advancements. Because of these changes, the styles of interactions of parents with their progeny will vary from decade to decade, from era to era.

It is well-known that India is composed of varying factors which impact upon each other to influence the styles of nurturance given to the progeny. The nurtured develops according to the different styles and standards of parenting used by the parents which impinge upon the processes in the chronological development of the nurtured.

The Indian society is well-known to be a heterogeneous society living in a vast number of differing ecologies with varying societal-norms. Various demographic influences change the Indian image dynamically. Societal-norms form the fulcrum of group behaviour in any society, creating various paradigms of interactive behaviour between the nurturant and the nurtured. Societies, however small or large, form themselves into communities, which within their own parameters subscribe to their own societal values and socio-religious beliefs, influencing the variations in the communities as to the perception of the nurturing process. The communities living adjacent to one another impinge upon each other in terms of their socio-cultural patterns. Members of these communities, therefore, share the same community identity and share similar sense of belongingness among the members of each of these given communities. Members of a community tend to share the same values and goals which results in a sense of cohesiveness, security and belongingness. These bases are what distinguish one community from another. For example, the *Bhils* of Madhya Pradesh are certainly quite different from the *Marwaris* of Gujarat in their societal values, their interactive patterns and more especially their patterns of communication and the values attached to each mode of behaviour. The *Bhils* live an elementary tribal life circumscribed by their specific geo-ecological areas and their relevant influences (Doshi, 1971). A member of this tribe lives in a homogenous pattern with the rest of the tribe, fiercely loyal to each other in order to preserve their identity as members of the community. Members of *Marwari* community, originating from Gujarat, are the major financiers and commercial group. This factor distinguishes them from other communities.

The *Marwaris* in India are scattered mostly on the west coast, the central and the eastern parts of India, namely Gujarat and Rajasthan on the west, Uttar Pradesh in the centre and West Bengal on the east coast, almost forming a chain linkage across the breadth of the Indian subcontinent. *Marwaris* are traditionally businessmen, traders and financiers. This makes them to spread out into different geographical areas. It is not necessary that the *Marwari* from one geo-ecological area share the same social values with the *Marwaris* of other geo-ecological areas. A *Marwari* might be a *munshi* in a little village and another *Marwari* might be a millionaire industrialist living in a metropolitan city. Because of these variations with regard to geo-ecological and socio-economic factors, and because of the interactive influences of various other variables, both conceptual and operational, the members of the *Marwari* community live a heterogeneous lifestyle. In the given world of changing ecologies, and differential occupational lifestyles, it is important to understand the variations in nurturing processes within specific communities. Still, there are specific socio-religious norms commonly shared by the members of a given community which distinguish it from any other community.

If the environs of a *Bhil* child and the *Marwari* child are examined simultaneously through the same lens, it will be obvious that there are various norms prevailing amongst these communities that give rise to differential perceptions which influence their styles of parenting. What brings about such differences? Chronologically they follow the same phylogenetic rules of development, but thereafter their attitudes, customs and values follow the ontogenetic innate tendencies, influenced by their specific geo and human ecologies. The phylogenetic evolutionary process gives a member of a human species the ability to walk, talk and interact in the same way as any other member of the species. Through a process of differentiation, however, an individual member of the species develops his own unique abilities and skills, such as being a sportsman or an intellectual as prompted by his inherent ontogenetic development, and following the epigenetic rules of development as influenced by the environment around him, both human and material (Baum. D, 2008). However, not all extraneous influences have similar effects. For instance, music might be rendered to two individuals, continuously under the same circumstances and in the same situation, yet it may be only one who is attracted to it, who is eager to learn music as a profession, while the other may not. In such a way, a member of human species affects and is affected by his environment differently from each other. In other words, there is no one individual exactly like the other in terms of responses to external influences even if they are fraternal twins. This differential pattern of behaviour is the result of a dynamic intermix of ontogenetic and extraneous variables impinging upon the individual, with different stimuli which work in different ecologies, in different manners of cognition and understanding the milieu in which these communities live.

Again, to take the example of the *Pangis* in Himachal Pradesh, the child lives a predictable routine lifestyle dealing with his own specific natural ecology, as did his forefathers before him (agrarian lifestyle as did his forefathers). A *Marwari* child used to living in various ecologies, on the contrary, lives a pattern of lifestyle quite different from thc *Pangis*.

Anyone *Marwari* child picked at random is different from one geo-ecological area to another even though they may be viewed through the same lens. Typically, a *Marwari* could be more cosmopolitan, more technologically oriented, and more worldly-wise through the influence of the social media. Therefore, the principles of "group variation" and "within group variation" are fundamental to an understanding of what makes for differing behavioural contexts. This statistical concept of variance among individual groups is foundational to understanding of why groups behave differently from each other and why members within each group also behave differently within the group. What strands hold these groups and individuals differentially apart? Logically, we must assume that there are inherent differences in the way they perceive, interpret, make deductions, and accommodate and assimilate their patterns of lifestyle with the rest. Attitudinally their value systems are different and the ways they perceive and interact with the rest of the world are also different. For instance, a tribal child will shy away from a city born and bred child, while a *Marwari* child who has mixed with crowds in market places and public places and such like will not be much affected by mixing with strangers. This is only one illustration out of a host of such possible illustrations when we consider that India is composed of several sub-cultures, several castes and several socio-economic groups which interact with each other distally or closely depending upon their geo-ecological habitat. If we take a combination of groups in India, from its various geographical areas, we find that there are further and further diffusions and fissions which again interact with specific habitats and varying human beings, their given habitat consisting of both human and material factors. India has 28 States and 9 Union Territories, with about 400 languages and dialects. This then creates a matrix pattern of interaction, based on the phylogenetic generic attributes, and if we view these differences in the families of the almost 1.25 billion people in

India, the differences are mind-boggling and yet each individual is an entity by himself or herself.

Given such varieties of ethnic groups in India, comparisons for understanding the variations are difficult to identify. A Rajasthani can be a *Rajput*, a *Marwari*, a *Brahmin*, a *Kumhar*, or a *Rehbari*, or a *Meo*. The latter follow Islam as their religion.

There are different types of identities for an Indian, such as identities based on caste, religion, region and ethnicity. Because of the different kinds of combinations of these identities, there are many forms of fissions in a specific group identified on the basis of either one of the different identity-giving attributes. For example, an ethnicity-based identity group is divided within it based on the sub-identities of region, religion and caste. All these differentiating factors impinge upon specific types of behaviours in the parenting practices.

In a given household the adults may react rigidly to the child's behaviour which may then get reflected in the bringing about of negative behaviour. Therefore, what is being attempted to display is that the rubric of attitudes, values and goals are constantly interacting with increased experiences. Values, attitudes and goals produce a heterogeneity of interactive qualities which grow in maturity to increase experiences. In this discussion, there is an attempt to stress these types of heterogeneous characteristics in the patterns of human behaviour. The emphasis is on the foundations of the parenting process, which is a prelude to specify the predominant parenting processes in the upbringing of the child. The book offers a general silhouette of parenting patterns and various ideological styles which get reflected in the exchanges and communications between the adult and the child and in the emotional and habitual behaviour of the parent and child.

The dynamic changes while unknown at any given time are dormant and can be revived on the slightest provocative cue. For example, a mother whose pattern of behaviour with the child is of constantly strict discipline depends upon other more stimulating modes when contingencies arise, such as when the child gives in to the mother's wishes because the former is interested in the bribe given by the mother.

Thus, the descriptions evident in the differences observed from one family to another gives rise to three major differentiating parenting styles and the corresponding differential responses given by the nurtured child. It is being said that there are three major parenting styles:

(i) Authoritarian,
(ii) Egalitarian, and
(iii) Third identifiable variable known, as *laissez faire* in character.

At the same time, an authoritarian style may also be authoritative and an egalitarian style may also be democratic and *laissez faire* style imply casualty in interaction between the nurturer and the nurtured.

2

Parenting Styles

Autocratic, Democratic, Laissez Faire and their Intermix

A parenting style is described as a pattern of behaviours of the parents towards their children. A particular parenting style involves a range of parent-child interactions which is continual as a habit and repeats itself into a pattern. Parenting practices are mechanisms through which parents directly help their children attain socialization goals (Khalakdina, 2011: xxx). Socialization goals include personality development goals, career achievement goals and cultural goals (Saraswati, T.S., 1999: 168). Stressing the concept of habit, we might say that the parenting process is habitual and, over a period of time, is goal-directed. The parenting process, when profiled with the personality of the parent, becomes a parenting style. Therefore, a parenting style is a specific set of continuous and habitual type of interaction that the parent has with the child depending on the personality of the parent.

Parenting style as a construct for the study of parent-child interactions was first proposed by Baumrind (1971, 1991). According to her, parenting style captures variations in parents' attempts to control and socialize their children. Parenting styles can be thought of as a contextual variable that moderates the relationship between specific parenting practices and specific developmental outcomes in the child. Normal parenting patterns revolve around issues of control or otherwise and their outcomes in the child. Baumrind has identified three typologies of parenting styles according to the level—high or low—of "demandingness" and "responsiveness" of the parents towards their children. These three types of parenting styles are:

(1) Indulgent,
(2) Authoritarian, and
(3) Authoritative.

Maccoby and Martin (1983) has identified a fourth type of parenting style, namely,

(4) Uninvolved.

(1) The Indulgent Parenting Style

The "indulgent" parenting style is also referred to as "permissive" or "non-directive". This is because much is left to the child's intelligence and cognition to be able to assess the situation and perform accordingly, so that, the child moves towards his or her perceived goals. The indulgent parents are more given towards allowing the child to use his cognitive abilities and capacities to direct himself/herself towards goal-perceived behaviour. The uninvolved parents are very high in nurturing their children, but are least bothered about the personality outcomes in children. They do not require their children to be responsible and self-controlled. They treat their children more like friends. Therefore, such parents can also be called "egalitarians." They take care to explain, persuade and get the child to come around, so to speak, to the parent's point of view, by being logical, and clear and giving injunctions which are possible within the realm of the child.

(2) The Authoritarian Parenting Style

The authoritarian parents are highly demanding and directive, but hardly responsive to the needs of the child. They set out rules of conduct and behaviour for their children who are pressurized to perform according to these rules as instructed by the parents. There is no discussion or explanation related to why the rules exist, and no negotiation with children over rules. The children have just to obey without questioning.

(3) The Authoritative Parenting Style

The authoritative parents are both demanding and responsive. The disciplinary methods used by authoritarian parents are supportive, rather than punitive. Authoritative parents provide explanations for the rules, listen to children's questions, and are even willing to negotiate a compromise. Parents are also less harsh in punishment, and more understanding and forgiving when children fail to meet their expectations. These parents do not set out to raise submissive, obedient individuals. They want their children to be responsible, appropriately assertive, cooperative, socially responsible and self-regulative (Baumrind, 1991: 62).

(4) The Uninvolved Parenting Style

Parents using this style are relatively uninvolved and do not insist on or punish a particular behaviour from the child. They are low in both responsiveness and demandingness. Such parents rarely communicate and are generally unresponsive to the needs of their children. While the child's essential needs are cared for, their emotional needs are neglected and, therefore, the child often feels rejected and unloved. The parenting style of these parents can be called *laissez faire* as they are leisurely attuned to the children's behaviour without too many pressures and injunctions, almost to the point of casual indifference.

Permissive or the *lassiez faire* parenting is often viewed as verging on neglect. Joanna Moorhead (2015) cites examples of this. One is that of a 41-year mother losing custody of her two sons by the ruling of the US High Court because she left them to their own devices for up to three hours when they came in from school while she chatted on her phone, took naps or was on her iPad. Another example of the ill-effect of the neglect of children by *laissez faire* parenting is the case of pupils as young as six found acting out violent and sexual scenes in the playground as reported by their teacher in her letter to parents. In this case, the children were simulating the actions from a computer game series called Grand Theft Auto, in which players took on the roles of underworld criminals. There are several instances reported in India of the gross neglect of children by the parents resulting in the children becoming delinquents and indulging in socially disapproved behaviours.

Parents are the main influence on a child's development. The nurturance of parents contributes to the physical as well as psychological development of the child. There are various socio-psychological aspects in the psychic development of a child. These include social competence, personality development, academic achievement etc. These are the goals towards which the parents nurture their children. The effect of the influence of the nurturance of the parents is considered to be most evident in the children during the chronological stage of adolescence.

Indian culture traditionally sets great importance on respect to the aged. This means that parents put great emphasis on acquiescence and obedience from their children. Modern society some times decries the erosion of these values. Yet social transformation in the present time may imply that parenting styles in India are also changing. For instance, expected compliance is often replaced with appeals to the child's reasoning and judgment.

Differences in parental styles bring about differences in the outcome in children in many respects. For example, children raised by authoritarian parents tend to be typically compliant, obedient, and proficient. However, they often suffer from depression, rate themselves lower on subjective happiness, are less socially competent and have low self-esteem (Nancy Darling, 1999). The children from authoritarian parents tend to perform moderately well in school and be uninvolved in problem behaviour. The children raised by authoritative parents fair well, are generally confident, capable and competent, socially well-adjusted and successful in life.

Authoritative parenting style is associated with positive developmental outcomes in children (Baumrind, 1971; Steinberg, Lamborn, Darling, Mounts, and Dornbusch, 1994). They perform well in schools (Dornbusch, Ritter, Leiderman, Roberts, and Fraleigh, 1987). They have higher self-esteem and psycho-social competence, and tend less to involve in problem behaviour (Maccoby and Martin, 1983; Buri, 1989; Lamborn, Mounts, Steinberg, and Dornbusch, 1991).

The authoritarian parenting style is considered to be conducive for optimal adjustment in children as it offers emotional support through responsiveness while at the same time establishing guidelines, limits and expectations through demandingness.

Children raised by permissive parents have poor self-regulation and self-control. They experience problems with authority and tend to perform poorly in school and in the work place. They are generally unhappy individual during their adult life. Children raised by the uninvolved parents tend to have worst outcomes in all areas of life such as emotional well-being, life-satisfaction, success in relationship, success at school and work etc. They generally lack self-control, have low self-esteem and tend to be less competent in social and practical life situations.

Parenting styles are not stand-alone psycho-sociological attributes. They are impinged upon by several extraneous variables which are dynamically evolving as the individual grows in experience. As said before, these outside experiences impinge upon the child's psyche, prompting him to modify his behavioural outputs, dependent of course upon the child's attitudes towards a particular object and towards particular goals which meets these objectives.

It stands to reason that within these adult-child parameters, the parent is the more powerful of the two since the parent has the wherewithal to care for the child without whose caring the child becomes rudderless. Therefore, if one views the fact that the children themselves have innate genetic styles of behaviour, the child may be known as a submissive child, as a rebellious child, or a careless child, as to the consequence of his behaviour, by most adults when they try to formulate concepts of their child's typical behaviour. So, when it is said that parents have a style of behaviour, it must be admitted that children themselves have their own ontogenetic skills of active and reactive behaviour (which may be negatively or positively toned, and which may change from time-to-time dependent on the cues or the provocation that the adult figure engenders). We give below a paradigm which attempts to put into inter-relation pattern the typical styles of the parent *vis-à-vis* the child.

Table 2.1: Patterns of Interaction between Parent and Child (Consistent and Inconsistent)

Parent	*Child*	*Heightened Value of Interaction*	*Effect of Consistent Parent-child Interaction*	*Effect of Inconsistent Parent-child Interaction*
Dominating (Authoritarian)	Dominating	+1	Confrontation	Divisiveness
Egalitarian (Democratic)	Egalitarian	0	Equilibrium	Harmony
Laissez faire (Indifferent)	*Laissez faire*	–1	Indifference	Exclusiveness
Dynamically varying interactive influences	Behaviour that changes from one pattern to another			

The above paradigm identifies three patterns of typical parenting styles and a fourth one which cannot be proactively qualified since it consists of an unknown set of dynamic interactions. These patterns are formed from a combination of genetic and ontogenetic inherent characteristics together with those formulated by the influence of the environment, namely attitudes, values and goal-directed behaviour of the adult towards the child. All these characteristics rest on a foundation of motivational directions and need-reduction theories (Maslow, 1948, 1970). The process by which the latter are internalized is through a process of relativity in interaction between a powerful adult and a less powerful child. The classical study of Lippit and White gives an identity to these types of behaviour from their classical experiment on leadership styles (Lewin, Lippit, and White, 1939). However, in operational terms, it is necessary to identify segmented activities in child-rearing. A child-rearing practice is the way in which the parent relates to a particular behaviour of the child like eating, sleeping, being toilet-trained and the child's reaction to disciplinary measures. There are several studies of child-rearing practices from many countries, especially the United States, Russia (Bronfenbrenner, 1970), the U.K., Japan (Bagley, Iwawaki and Young (1983) and China (Biggs, 1992) and smaller studies using similar formats in India. Put together, they contribute to discerning different styles of parenting, each style implying a more or less persistent pattern of behaviour in the interaction of the parent with the child. In the paradigm above, we have taken the types experimented upon by Lippit and White to indicate three identifiable patterns in child-rearing. For example, a mother who constantly threatens the child in disciplining is typically authoritarian using, as Sears (1951) puts it, punishment techniques which are constantly reinforced, becoming a pattern of negative reinforcement. On the other hand, in getting the child to accomplish a certain activity, the parent will use a disciplinary technique called "love-oriented" or "positive" reinforcement. In cases where the parent uses neither the positive "love-oriented" technique nor the negative punishment-based technique, the parent is considered casual in her parenting practice. We use the term *"laissez faire"* to characterize the parenting style of such parents.

Parenting is not a one-sided activity, but an inter-related activity. The parent communicates a type of behaviour which is psychologically oriented that the child should perform. The child either acquiesces in or does not. Sometimes, there will be repeated non-compliance on the part of the child. This may amount to confrontation as the child grows older. However, as is well-known, intermittent conditioning eventually move the child along the pathways determined by the parent as the child has no experience in alternative methods of behaviour except to protest and to disobey. Over-time, if the parents' behaviour is consistently authoritative, the child learns to submit. But, otherwise, if both have dominating personalities, there is likely to be constant confrontation. As the child grows older into adolescence and young adulthood, he might behave somewhat unexpectedly. His behaviour may take the form of protest against parental dictates and even open rebellion against parental authority. If the adolescent has a strong character, the adolescent might find his own ways of behaving in order to achieve his own perceived goals, resisting if needed parental dictates.

The theories of parenting and parenting styles are mainly concentrated on practices of how to care for children through their growing years and deal with such aspects as weaning, toilet training, solid-feeding, disciplining and inculcating habits and values. The parental and child behaviours in the theories follow a route, which are in the main theoretically circumscribed. For instance, need-reduction theory is based upon the child's own innate direction of behaviour arising from the unconscious. There was little emphasis on the interaction at the communication levels between the parent and the child and, as is happening now-a-days, seeking the advice of pediatricians and attuning themselves to childcare topics that appear in social media.

3
Sources of Parenting Behaviour

Parents do not grow-up to be adults suddenly. They go through a process of childhood before reaching adulthood. When they have their own children, they usually take on the responsibility of parenting utilizing their own experiences when they themselves were children. The yearning to bear one's own child and to nurture him/her till adulthood is a natural inherent feeling of an individual who becomes a parent. In the Indian context this feeling is called *"mamata"*. The need to have one's own children is materialized almost always after marriage takes place. At times, children are also born even without the marriage. Greater numbers of pre-marital conceptions is a recent trend in India. In recent times, there is a greater number of unmarried adult females in India because of the phenomenon of the female marriage squeeze and also because of the prolongation of marriage or even choosing to remain single as women seek greater freedom to opt for careers in professions which enhance their status. The female marriage squeeze is the result of the rapid increase in the population and the subsequent increase in cohort size and the non-availability of grooms because of the problem of dowry (Bhat and Shiva, 1999). When there are more unmarried females, there tends to be sex out of marriage and conceptions out of marriage. The children born without marriage are not simply abandoned. The mothers try their maximum to take care of them. If any exception to this occurs, it might be because of reasons other than the absence of the biological yearning to care for one's young. Children out of wedlock may be abandoned because of social stigma or utter financial incapability of the mother. But these factors are largely not relevant in the case of the educated and professionally oriented adult females who choose to be single. The biological parents nurture their children with great emotional bonding. In all cases it is not essential that parents should have biological children. Now-a-days even if not married, single women adopt children. This is perhaps because of an innate feeling of motherliness of adult females as they have an epigenetically developed maternal propensity to nurture the young of the species. This explains why some of the adult females who, because of genetic factors (impotency, infertility), cannot biologically produce children, adopt children and nurture them. They too use different parenting styles based on their own childhood experiences as also by observing parenting practices of others. There are still others who cannot afford bringing up children when children are conceived out of wedlock. These children are usually given up for adoption or put into foster homes or under institutional care. This trend is a recourse that parents have taken to in the last few decades in India. In the earlier days, giving up children for adoption by others or for institutional care hardly existed because of the prevalence of the joint family system. In a joint family the child was taken care of not only by the biological parents, but by everybody else in the large joint family. In the joint family system, therefore, child care was not a problem even if the parents of the child were no longer living or could no longer take care of the child. The situation has largely changed in modern times as the joint family system is disappearing. Currently, with the increasing numbers of the nuclear families, the biological parents have to take up full responsibility of nurturance and socialization of their own young.

In the process of socializing or parenting the young, most Indian parents use their own childhood experiences, recalling the parenting practices of their own parents. They also take advice from relatives and neighbours or even from the social media. The habit of reading books and taking professional advice was not in the repertoire of the traditionally-oriented parents, except that a few educated used the famous Doctor Spock's advice. Most of the traditionally oriented parents in India follow the community customs and social values in the parenting of their young.

In the modern world, though the family has underwent transformation in its structure, from the joint to extended, and to nuclear family—its function as an institution remains the same as before. It still mostly determines the development of individuals. It still is the major source of nurturance, emotional bonding and socialization. However, the structural change in the family and the underlying factors that brought about this change, have affected parental choices and preferences in the process of socializing their children. Modern day parents use a variety of sources such as educational books on child-rearing and child-care and audio and visual media and social media in gaining knowledge about appropriate parenting practices. The spread of education and information has given rise to a number of theoretical understandings on how best to rear and guide children and on the strategies used by the parents in their parenting styles. Thus, in the modern world, the important sources of parenting of children are:

(i) One's own parental upbringing; and
(ii) Observation of parental upbringing from friends and social media.

However, the most important factor that determines the style of parenting is the personality of the parent. It is important to note what concepts lie behind the term personality. A personality is expressed in a person's behaviour. There are different sources of behaviour of a person. The first is behaviour arising from consciousness; the second is the unconscious areas of volition; and the third and perhaps the deepest influence is the parents' own needs, motivations and goals. All of these impinge upon the parenting practices and styles. The source of conscious perceptions of what should be done to a child in a given situation is dependent upon the deliberate pathways the parent takes to monitor and guide the child. Young mothers who are relatively inexperienced in parenting might use that style which is most appealing to herself. During parenting, the child, depends upon the adult for his needs in the early stages of growth. However, gradually the child, as he grows up chronologically, moves away from this dependency relationship with the parent as he/she tries to use his/her own independent style of behaviour. At this time, the conscious efforts of the parent begin to dwindle down and then get attritioned over a period of time. This happens because the child gains in maturity and accumulates experiences which give him a sense of adequacy and individuality in coping with his own needs. Thus, the early years are those when mothers make conscious efforts in their interaction with the child to direct and guide him/her in their daily lives. For example, with the preschool child, the mother repeatedly voices familiar jingles like "this is the way we wash our face, early in the morning", a type of voice and, articulation which the child repeats and gradually internalizes rhythmically. However, these expressions are idiomatic in the culture in which the child's family lives. This directive repetition does not happen automatically. The parent consciously has to persuade, cajole and promise rewards to the child in order to get the child to repeat these jingles. This is based on the long-term goals of getting the child to internalize the auditory noise created by the jingles. Thus, the auditory action eventually becomes part of the behavioural repertoire of the growing child. In India, there are a variety of sub-cultures, and correspondingly a tremendous number of idiomatic expressions, which are used as expressive ideations of what the intention of the adult is. Each culture has its idiomatic frame like the little poem *"incy wincy makada"* (a takeoff on *incy wincy spider* in the English nursery rhyme). This repetitive imitative behaviour does not happen automatically. Beneath this conscious efforts are two conceptual frames, namely, *reinforcement* and *conditioning*. In other words repeated reinforcement with repetitive action and words tends to bring about imitative behaviour in the child.

Another aspect is the unconscious behaviour. This aspect is one that is deeply recessed in the individual's past experiences which are usually suppressed in the unconscious. Repressed into this unconscious are the memories of those experiences which are usually traumatic, negative or unpleasant. Such experiences cannot be expressed in socially approved expressions. The suppressed experiences are usually in contradiction with societal norms. Socially disapproved experiences occur in everyday experiences, but since they are anti-societal or non-normative, they are usually suppressed into the unconscious of which the conscious layer of the human psyche is unaware of. This repression is unknown unless and until something similar, a duplicate of the stimulus which provoked the undesirable ideation, reappears in the environment. Frequently, realizing the explosive nature of the negative experiences, the parent represses the influence of such experiences in her parenting process. For example, in her childhood she may have had a very negative and harsh step-mother. As she grows up, she deliberately try to banish all her experiences related to her interactions with her stepmother and thus represses them into the innermost layer of the unconscious. This is a simplistic operational explanation of an unconscious mode of behaviour based on the psycho-analytical theory of Freud [1990, 1953], followed on by neo-Freudians.

Most of the individuals' ideations, imaginations, curiosity and such like movements in parental behaviour evolve from the basic, normal stimuli, which form the larger context of ideations. The acquisition of these experiences in a chained logical manner is set in the brain for future linkages. For example, a physical injury is a stimulus and the response to it triggers a chain of reactions. An internal mental stimulus may be the remembrance of one's wedding day. This positive experience is repeated wherein a pleasant feeling pervades the individual, indicative of pleasure, which feelings are evoked repeatedly. Stimuli can, therefore, be both positive and negative and responses are usually in the same direction. The individual in remembrance evokes a set of pleasurable ideations which then occur and re-occur when they are pleasurable. A painful memory, when it re-occurs, is an ideation which is repeated from memory. Most parental style is built around such stimuli which evoke responses from the child in like manner and does not depend upon repeated requests or injunctions. A little detailing as given in the stimulus-response theory indicates that stimuli can be qualitative. It can be conditioned, and it can be intermittent. These qualifications of a stimulus in fact tend to evoke stronger responses which, therefore, become part of the interactive processes between the parent and the child, and become a more or less permanent characteristic behaviour of the child towards cues in the environment, whether emanating from an adult individual or from the environment. These ideations are based on the theories of Hall and Watson, Freud's theory of psychoanalysis and the topological conceptualization of Kurt Lewin (Lewin, 1936). The topological theory assumes that there are spaces within the brain where regions are formed which are regions of habit and of social value. They change dynamically as and when stimuli change. The most predominantly evolving ideation in adolescents revolves around heterosexual relationships. Usually after marriage and the bearing of children, the sets of ideations attach themselves to a new set of behavioural operations. There are forces within the environment, emanating both from the human and material sources, which attempt to occupy prominent field spaces in the mental make-up of the brain structure, which transform into expressive behaviour and form strong habits and values, some of them difficult to eradicate. Those difficult to eradicate are ideationally situated at the central focus of brain ideation and are called core behaviours or centrifugal in nature. Those ideations which are peripheral can appear and disappear as unstable elements. For example, adolescents want to continue to listen to a pop music which most parents want their children to desist from. Food habits are difficult to change and, therefore, tend to remain constant. On the periphery of the brain structure are peripheral values and habits which are priority at some times and not priority at other times.

That means the peripheral values and habits dynamically change as the growing individual goes through life experiences, changing his habits, his attractions and future behaviour, unlike core habits which, as said before, are unlikely to change, as for instance, socio-religious habits. These are the personality determinants which influence the behaviour as the child gathers more experiences. They are triggered off by the brain structure and are, therefore, personality determinants.

There are genetic factors influencing the personality traits, apart from the environmental factors. The latter consists of both the shared and the non-shared (the unique) environments. The parenting practice is a shared environment of the siblings. The peer group is an example of the non-shared or unique environment of a growing individual. According to the behaviour studies of adult personality, the genes and unique environment are important influences in the development of personality, but the share environment plays lesser role in the personality development (Essence, 1990).

Besides these personality determinants, there are cues emanating from the environment. These are cues emanating from the environment such as the human ecology, environmental climatic factors, i.e., geo-ecology, and community attributes (Jodhka, 1999).

Psychologically speaking, the individual raised in a culture is parented to conform to the norms of his culture and any violation of the norms is against normally expected behaviour. It is also well-known that the individual employs several defence mechanisms (Freud, 1946) in order to repress socially disapproved behaviour, outrageous feelings, attitudes and values and to express himself or herself in terms of the values and attitudes of the society in which the child lives. Any transgression brings in conflict between the child and his environment. For example, in life one comes across many people whom one does not like and even in situations where one intensely dislike the other, in public places, where social norms are prevalent, these negative emotions are not expressed in behaviour. The individual harbouring such negative emotions behaves in a pretentiously socially approved manner, although internally what the individual would like to say is that "I hate you, I cannot stand you".*A follow-on class of ideations, which individuals experience, are related to need-reduction theories (Allport, 1954), theory of values and Maslow's theory of the hierarchy of needs (Maslow, 1943). These three theories taken together imply that human beings whether the parent or child, have a set of needs, changing or unchanging.

According to Maslow, the needs are both primary and secondary. Most adults while bringing up their children lay emphasis on these needs, especially, the primary needs which they attempt to guide the child towards. The primary needs include food, shelter and clothing. The secondary needs are the need for healthcare, education, and the need for achievement and self-esteem. There are also need for companionship and the need to compete with peer groups. In the parenting milieu, however, the need for love and care from the bonding parent is the most overriding. Secondary needs are those which are relative to the individual who is attached to the child in such a way that the child feels the need to be in close proximity with the caring parent. There are personal needs like the need for affiliation, for recognition, for security, for dependency, for stability, for freedom, and such like (Maslow, 1970). In the Indian situation, given the large proportion that lives below the poverty line, the primary needs are of high priority. When these are met, secondary needs follow closely, especially the needs for affiliation and belongingness with its attendant needs for safety and security. When primary needs are satisfied, then the secondary needs occupy a priority place depending upon the need perception of the perceiver and the internal assessment of the person experiencing these needs. A secondary need may be, and most often is, a need for affiliation as human beings do not wish to live alone but in a society of members and, therefore, needs to feel a sense of affiliation being met, for example, friendship ties. Most adults wish their children to achieve.

* For a fuller description of these theories, refer Hall, Lindzey and Campbell, 1998; Also read M. Khalakdina, 2012.

During the lifetime of childhood, they impress upon the child the need to achieve in life with different kinds of strengths of inputs at different times. In school, the need for achievement is to obtain high ranks. After finishing school, the parents motivate the child to study towards a profession and become somebody noteworthy among his or her companions. Under all conditions, however, a conscious or unconscious behaviour on the part of the parent reinforces the growing child along the pathway perceived by the parent. In the parents' behaviour with the child, there is an underlying notation of the concept of goal-fulfilment, according to the aspirations of the parenting adult. Therefore, we view the needs of the parent and child simultaneously where the primary needs are similar, but from then on, the secondary needs are disparate depending upon the differing priorities and perceptions of the adult and the child. The tendency is that the secondary needs change dynamically according to the perceived need of the influencing adult, namely, the parent.

All ideations stored in the memory are not entirely pleasant at one and the same time. Some may have negative and perhaps extremely regressive or aggressive connotations. For example, a mother, who in her childhood has been severally beaten several times for disobedience, represses the experience and tries her best not to be tempted to use such disciplinary measures with her own progeny. We some times find parenting adults who have experienced excessive rigidity in their own upbringing might not reproduce the same in their children in an autocratic way of communication. This is simply because they are being sensitive to the harm it can do to a growing child. They, therefore, deviate from the pathway of negative influence (Miller, 1944, 1959). On the other hand, if the parent in her childhood had been told and insisted on by her mother that the right way to bring up a child is through a negative regimen, she might attempt this in her own strategies with her own child.

Another example is that of little children being brought up in war-torn areas with the constant fear of bombing and seeing people around them dying horrible deaths which cannot be erased from the child's memory so that in any similar repetitive situations, they might display some traumatic behaviour. In extreme cases, behaviour might break down into hysterical avoidance of the parents' insistence.

While there are many theories of personality, and examples of attendant behaviour, the most relevant bases of behaviour, as exemplified above, are the theories of Stimulus-Response (Miller, 1948), reinforcement (Skinner, 1974), conditioning (Bandura, 1977) and the various branches of psycho-analytical theories, chief among them being the theory of influence of psycho-somatic aberrations (Jung, 1961; Fraud, 1946). Behaviour is identified in most personal interactive situations as being normal as there are several standards of normality. It is difficult to predict whether the adult parent's behaviour arises from the conscious or an unconscious source. Consciously, the adult is not aware of the reinforcement she received in her own childbood, but it has such a telling effect on the parent's behaviour that, on the slightest cue, it emerges emotionally from out of the parent's repressed mental storehouse of negative behaviour.

A more telling impact on the child is the adult's own aspirations, values and goals which may be packaged as a group of needs towards which the child is motivated on cues from the parent.

Table 3.1 : Sources of Parental attitude toward child and related processes and results.

Source	*The Process*	*The end-result*
Past learned behaviour	The deliberate attempt to consciously remember and rehearse again experiences from childhood that are pleasant and to avoid which are unpleasant.	The child is brought up as a model inherited by the adult from her or his own upbringing.
The current social norms	The conscious attempt to instil the behaviour that is acceptable in society by using reinforcement techniques and assessing the need for unconsciously motivated behaviour directed towards the child.	The child self-selectively uses socially approved behaviour and tries to negate unconsciously those which are not conducive to his perceived goal attainment.

(Contd.)

Source	*The Process*	*The end-result*
The evolution of behaviour towards goal-attainment	Adults live their lives with goals in mind. They use techniques to urge the child to behave according to the perceived goals which they expect the child to internalize.	The result is a combination of the characteristic habits of the adult and the child's own inherent characteristics. Along these dimensions the goal-achievement is related to parental perception, the child's perception and the parental and child's needs, thus making a composite of the movement towards perceived, desired end-behaviour of the child.

However, at any one time, none of these sources are mutually exclusive. There are always shades of the others. For example, the conscious behaviour some times gets overlaid with some strands of the unconscious. The quantity of overlap is evoked by the child's own ability, goals, and the needs towards which these goals are directed, which the child uses selectively from the parental goals presented to the individual child. They may be quite different from that expressed by the adult who may be barriered by confrontation and controversy, more especially noticeable in the adolescent years of the child, the early years being years of more susceptibility to adult communication, guidance and imitation by learning from adult behaviour. None of these types of behaviour can be perceivably separated from any others. It is like a vortex of different volumes, continuing one upon the other, some shortened by the dynamics of the other and some others lengthened by the persistence of goal-directed behaviour. It is not always necessary that there is a compliant response from the child towards the goal-directed behaviour of the parent. This is especially true during adolescence and often leads to estrangement between the two generations.

In the whole repertoire of behaviour, both emanating from the parent and incorporated by the child, is the concept of motivation of the child. Motivation is closely allied to need, because it then becomes the propelling force towards urging the individual to move in a specific direction of goal-directed behaviour. Motivation does not arise out of nothing. The individual has to be interested, the individual needs to have desire to achieve and the individual needs to work towards the achievement. This applies to both the parent and the child. A mother who is highly motivated to want her child to be a well-known surgeon or a lawyer or to get into a highly respected well-paying situation, might do all that she can, even using all the different parenting styles, and yet the child may be unmotivated, perhaps because the child himself or herself is not at all attuned to these technologically based professions, but would like to be an artist.

What is motivation therefore? Motivation arises from the well of needs, especially the unfulfilled needs of the adults, which impinge on the child and internally persuades the child to move along that pathway directed by the adult to whom the child is closely bonded. True, the adult may keep intact the needs she had learned from her own childhood, as for instance her mother having communicated to her during her childhood that she should not lie and she should not behave dishonestly. These two types of images the adult imbibes and transfers it to her child during the parenting process. The child may be motivated by the parent whereby the child is offered incentives to go along the pathway indicated by her parent. The concept of motivation is what makes human beings progressive in their behaviour during the chronological growth of mental capacity. Motivation, of course, is a feeling dependent upon a need. "The greater the need, the greater is the motivation to desire to fulfil the need" (Atkinson, 1958). A child in the primary school age is motivated to play only with the same sex, but during the adolescence, he or she would like to be in the company of the opposite sex also. These changes, therefore, are not only chronologically propelled, but are also dependent upon the force of the mother's need *vis-à-vis* the force of the child's need, and more often than not the parents needs motivate the child to fulfil the former's aspirations. If the child is subservient to the mother's needs, he will willingly follow the pathway indicated by the mother, but if he experiences other competing needs, he will rebel and find ways and means of getting out of the pathway delineated by the adult parent.

We see this operating in real life situations when parents say with great surprise and concern when the child behaves in a disorderly manner, "but I have always brought him up to be honest and disciplined, and not disobedient and indisciplined." However, the child is an entity in and of himself. While he might be biologically related to the adult, he grows up developing his own set of needs, which he may retain in spite of the adult's expressed goal for him. The child might face an inward struggle with different competing needs. He might store in memory his mother's aspirations, his friend's aspirations and the needs of others dear to him at the same time. If he has a changeable nature, he might move from one set to another. Thus, like a rubric, one need impinges upon the other and are dynamically rotated till the grown up child comes to set-upon a certain patterned behaviour which then becomes his own style, and eventually if and when he produces a family he will tend to use those styles which he learned from his childhood. At times, he behaves like an angel and, at other times, he moves away from the adult-directed path and moves on his own pathway even if it is contrary to what the parenting adult has conveyed to him. Unfortunately, unlike the lower mammals, the human being's behaviour is dynamically changeable, and, therefore, in many ways unpredictable. Thus child at times may behave in an unpredictable manner (and it is only through repeated instigations that the child complies with the parent's directive, part of the reason being that the child does not have the same emotive directions as does the parent). Often, the adult who parents the child mistakenly thinks that what the child has been taught to become, he will eventually become. For the child has its own mind and, as is said before, his own needs which could come in clash with those of his parents. He has the cueacuity to unload what is in the parent's mind in a given situation, to reassess what he has unloaded as a pattern, and to find a pathway as to how he can bypass them or how he can limit them. This is very commonly seen in the young child's behaviour who, if the mother, is negligent, indifferent or *laissez faire,* would keep distracting his mother's attention from other things so that her focus is on what he is saying or doing. At other times, the child is unable to fathom what is going on in the mind of the adult and he thus begins to negotiate. If there is a slab of chocolate and the child is a *chocoholic*, he cannot resist wanting the whole. He, therefore, say to the adult whom he knows will not give him the whole chocolate, "give me a small piece and then I go outside to play and come back, give me another piece", or, he might say, "you always tell me I do not keep my clothes and toys in order, so if I do that, will you give me a large piece of chocolate?" Or, if he has siblings, close to his age, who also like chocolates, he might diligently watch what proportion of the chocolate the others are getting and might create a tantrum because he thinks it is unfair if they get a larger portion. The child is a sharp negotiator and as he grows older, he finds ways and means of coding, decoding his parents' communication or behaviour, and brings up his own characteristics of behaviour to meet his needs, even though they do not coincide with that of the parent.

These illustrations are mainly to indicate the dynamic changes that occur in the child's mind as a response to the adult's directions, whether authoritarian or egalitarian or *liassez faire*. It is possible that he has a set of strong genes for need-fulfilment than do the other children in the family and, therefore, the adult has to treat him differently from the other siblings. For example, his younger brother might be content with a little piece of chocolate as his personality is submissive and compliant, but the older sibling will insist on a larger share just because, he says, I am older than he is and, therefore, I need more chocolate. This type of reasoning begins in the young child in the cognitive years of formal operations (Piaget and Inhelder, 1969). The child, therefore, attempts to put "two and two together" to his own advantage. Very often adults around him, find this type of behaviour as being precocious, meaning more mature than the age warrants. This kind of mature behaviour is quite acceptable in child behaviour as it cannot be assumed that there are rigid progress lines of chronological maturity. A child of six, for instance, might exhibit more mature behaviour than his brother who is a couple of years older. In fact, when viewed from the theories of personality, it can be seen that the child will show such behaviour when he is of a certain age (cognitive informal pre-operational stage). It is not necessary that these occur rigidly in the framework of a child's growth in terms of these attributes and chronological age. Much depends upon the intelligent and emotional maturity of the child. On the other hand, some children may have such poor concept formation, abilities that they are unable to catch up with the cue intensity of others even if they are of their own age. It has been digressed in earlier discussions to indicate that although certain known patterns of pathways of behaviour might exist, the child is an unknown entity and may, suddenly, at any given time change his behaviour and put the adult into perplexity. The adult usually thinks, "if I teach my child such and such, repeatedly rewarding his behaviour, he will behave the way I perceive he should." This may not happen. The child may aggressively behave in an opposite manner. Such examples abound in the stages of pre-adolescence and adolescence where the adult unintentionally forgets that her child is very susceptible to peer group pressures. So, she may suddenly find that all her painstaking efforts towards a directed behaviour draw a complete blank from her child, who says, "But all my friends do it, so I want to do the same way", and, therefore, he creates the situation which is either sulking, being non-communicative, sitting grossly in a corner, refusing to eat, even though he is offered his favourite food item. The child keeps persisting in this kind of behaviour till finally the parenting adult lets down the veil of rigidity and begins to compromise with him. In the West, since it is forbidden to physically punish a child, no matter which class or group, the most commonly used way to punish a child is to deprive him of his favourite item and have to take "time off", namely excluded "for a period of time from interaction with others". The child might cry, might whimper, might sob himself to sleep and the mother can do one or two things. Either give in to the child's wishes or let him sob for long times although it pains her a great deal. Children have different degrees of sensitivities. The long sobbing and long non-forgiveness by the parent might be construed by him as a traumatic incident for him. When a similar occasion occurs that might give rise to such similar impasse. He has a high cue grasp of the past incident and has a high cue grasp that it might occur again and so he quickly changes the topic and diverts the adult's mind so that the incident does not recur. Children are full of alternative ways of behaviour and consciously or unconsciously, if rational and reasonable in their personality make-up, can often find ruses to take the adult's mind off to focus on his persistent behaviour. Before we go on to explain parenting styles, we must understand the foundational shifting strands of sources of parenting, where one arises and the other falls, but always and continuously in a dynamic fashion and in such ways that often the adult is unable to reason out why this kind of reactive behaviour of the child occurs. Thus, foundational sources can be at one and the same time somewhat consciously and somewhat unconsciously motivated; more unconscious than conscious, more highly stimulated by the parental need, or if the child is aggressive, is more on the basis of the child's needs. These are not silent modes of action. They are also accompanied by language modes, whether verbal or body language, but such body and verbal language expresses an emotion which is either confrontational or acquiescent towards which the adult gravitates and, therefore, the parent uses one or both modes in different strengths to direct the child's pathway. These are also familiar patterns. We often see the adult sitting with the child at his dinner trying to get the child to eat when she knows very well that he is difficult to feed and so the adult would rack the brains to think of all kinds of ways to distract his attention on the food while she is feeding him consciously, but unconsciously makes him towards eating his meal by using play methods, reading a book or dramatizing a situation so that the child is directed towards eating his food automatically without the adverse feeling he initially had.

Major Sources of Determinants

There are two major sources that emanate from the parenting nexus. These may be categorized under two general headings as,

(a) Personal determinants, and
(b) Situational determinants.

In the nexus of personal determinants, the most significant is the close bonding between the parent and the child, starting with the parameters of nurturance. These give further rise to additive personal characteristics of the parenting adult. Sometimes, the parent may be over-indulgent, over-protective, over-rigid and even overly lax. That is, within this nexus of bonding, there is quick crossing over, from time-to-time between strong characteristics of this type and the weak characteristics of the same type. For example, an over-protective parent may at times be lax. An over-indulgent parent may at times be strict about indulgence. Therefore, like any other characteristics of human nature, there are always dimensions that are positive and negative, dimensions that are strong and weak and dimensions that are characterless. Parenting given in orphanages is an example of the lack of maternal bonding between the parent and the child. Thus, situational determinants are those which influence these personal determinants. A parent might want to be over-indulgent, but circumstances prevent her from doing so. She might want to be over-protective, but may not be able to do so as she lives in a joint family or is divorced from her husband and is a single parent. These are situational determinants which might modify a parent's characteristics, without being apparent to her. For example, the situation of being a single mother prevents her from giving the kind of protectiveness usually given by the father of the child, namely the husband. She has to manage singly, meeting with different kinds of situational determinants over which she has no control. Therefore, the controlling environment is tangential to the personality input that the mother wishes to use, and thereby the intended effect does not occur.

Personal Determinants

What are the further sources of personal determinants? For this, we turn to the parameters of the genome map. The Genome contains all of the biological information of an individual member of a species. Genome is a biological set of nuclei which chemically occur in combination due to orthogenetic factors in the human being. Each set of factors influences organisms differentially from each other (Ridley, 2006). As regards the human beings, the most intricate formulation is in the brain. Any debilitation or shortfall in the functions of the brain system leads to shortfalls in the performance of normal mental functions. The system that regulates growth in the brain is the pituitary hypothalamus and the hormonic system. The hypothalamus in the human brain control human body adjustments according to external and internal cues. It regulates body temperature, hunger, thirst, and sexual activity, goal-seeking behaviour, endocrine functions, affective (emotional) behaviour, and the activity which is the prime function of the visceral nervous system. The major aspects of the brain which control behaviour are vestibular nuclei, which control reflexes of the skeletal and muscular system, and *cerebral cortex,* a sheet of neural tissue that is the outermost layer of the cerebrum of the brain, which plays a key role in memory, attention, perceptual awareness, thought, language, and consciousness.

The cerebrum, the cortex, the cerebellum and the hypothalamus system work in conjunction with a set of connective tissues called neurons. Synapses are chemical transmitters which are connected through these sets of neurons which carry messages from the sensory organs to the brain where it is decoded and sent back to the sensory organs for action and/or reaction (Penfield and Rasmussen, 1950).

The personal determinants of any one individual is vastly different from those of another individual, simply because of the various settings of the neurons and because of the formation of *synapses,* the connective tissues and DNAs which are vastly different from one individual to another. There is no accurate analysis of what makes for an aggressive personality or a submissive personality or any of the types that are perceived by the outer world. The DNA mapping system has taken high significance in the past century and it has speeded up the analysis of complex genetic traits of different mammals. We still do not know the one-to-one relationship between the mind and the triggering of cellular positions in the brain. For the human mind is more an intellectual cognitive system and rests on its own DNA patterning of thinking, feeling and doing. It is most important in the understanding of deranged behaviour like schizophrenia, mental retardation and such like mental diseases. Normally, the structures of the make-up of the brain are similar from one to another and the functions follow a regulative pathway of the mind. Thus, we see that an individual is in control of the thought processes of creativity and of innovativeness in the mankind's evolution.

Environmental/situational determinants are more or less static like flora and fauna and of course, the advance of technology, has set-up situations which no longer depend entirely upon the creativity of the mind but upon what it has already created, and will continue to progress creating, namely advanced and sophisticated technology. Already we are aware of the hacking system in computers which helps in the long-range spying into private homes, of obtaining written information without having to scan books, and accessing materials straightaway from electronic gadgets and speedy social media. However, this type of development is happening more especially in urbanized metropolitan areas where significant situational determinants change rapidly and dynamically. However, in those areas, remotely touched or not touched at all by technology, life tends to remain similar from one generation to another. If we view the behaviour of the human beings, whether adult or child, it is observable that the tribal child, the rural child, the hill child, the fishermen's child have very little knowledge of technology or its advancement and, therefore, are relatively untouched in their habitual ways of behaviour. In other words, situational determinants are not dynamic. In such ecologies, where the situation remains more or less the same overtime, the flora, fauna and climatic changes do not affect much the change of behaviour of human beings living in those environs. In these relatively untouched areas, it is easy to predict what habits and values and ways of living are systemic, for they are ingrained in the living life of the communities. These communities are tribals and people who belong to the fragile populations like *Dalits* and traditional women. They are little affected by what is happening in urban metropolitan areas. True, as geographical transitions take place, where there is movement, even though gradual from rural to urban, where the ruralite further congests urban slums, the fact remains that differences will continue to exist as all facets of geo-ecological life will move from simple to complex, through one generation to another. This is observable in one's life time. Children teach their parents about the intricacies of the computer, the different varieties of cellular and even coded information. Therefore, what we say today of parenting styles, for example, will not be so as the years go on, as there seems to be a continuing hiatus between one and the next generation. Children now-a-days, especially the young adolescent and the young adult, are less prone to be influenced by parenting styles than what happened a few decades ago. This is so because there is an increasing influence of knowledge from the technological world and from social media.

When all the genes are arranged in a mapping system, they indicate the total specific organism. The biological information contained in a genome is encoded in its DNA and is divided into discrete units called genes. Genes are codes for proteins that attach to the genome at the appropriate positions and they switch on a series of reactions called gene expression.

Each individual has a particular set of chromosomes, in a unique fashion differentiated from others. Some of these chromosomes are inherited, some are dominant, some are suppressed and some appear indifferently, depending upon the mental acumen of the person based upon the brain cells that are formulated by these chromosomes. All brains have the same physiological structure, but the make-up that controls the intellect, memory, imaging, visual activity and the power to make decisions or otherwise emanate from special configurations of the chromosomes. Epigenesis is that area of knowledge that takes into account the fact that all human beings, as members of a specific species think, feel and act in a some what similar fashion, given the same essential phylogenetic structures. Each human being takes his specific epigenetic root to arrive at his goal, or at least attempt to arrive at his goal. A parent, for instance, might try very hard to discipline a hyperactive child, but if he or she is also hyperkinetic, then the parental characteristics tend to reinforce the child's hyperactivity. We have often seen this exhibited in nervous and excitable mothers who are alert to every movement of their child as the child moves in quick succession from one activity to another, displaying a hyperactive physio-emotional characteristic. How do we know this? In simple terms, we say that the probability of epigenetic activity will tend to activate the human being, who possesses these chromosomes in overabundance, to that which is normally known. This is the same explanation that we can give for children who are mentally retarded. If there is also some mental retardation in the parent, it tends to, on a probabilistic basis, be inherited by the biological child. In more acute forms, this is visible in diseases that are known to be genetically inherited such as diabetics, high blood pressure and the propensity towards cancer and in many cases, heart diseases. These chromosomes are, so to speak, lurking in the genome map and can be activated on pressure either from the individual or from the environment. Therefore, there are two distinguishing factors that describe the chromosomic arrangement within each individual's brain, which then tends to direct and dictate his ability such as IQ, the tendency to be lethargic, that is to react in a slow manner to the cues emanating from the environment, human or material. This probabilistic genesis is present in each individual and can be potentialised or depressed depending upon the individual's physiological and emotional experiences.

As we said, all of us have chromosomic arrangements, some of which are inherited, but much of it lies within the capacity of the mind or the will of the individual. What relates the mind and the will to the brain is well-accepted. But how this relationship operates in the living human being is still not yet fully explainable by the neurosciences. We do know, however, that brain damage causes disruption in the normal functional ability of the individual. Studies of the examination of foetuses reveal that brain retardation causes feeble physiological reactions of the newborn. This genome variation belongs to the area of the pool of the genomes that formulate one individual as being different from the other. We term these inherent functionalities or dysfunctionalities as personal determinants (Erikson, 1968).

All men can walk, talk and think and, therefore, the functionality of the physiognomy is the same. It is the extent to which it is used, not used, depressed or elevated, that makes for one individual being different from another. The theory of individual differences draws on the result of this genetic mapping of an individual. However, each individual operates in a different manner although phylogenetically he or she is like any other individual. Phylogenies is the evolutionary development of common characteristics of a given species, such as a fish can swim automatically while monkeys can climb trees automatically, and humans cannot swim and climb trees automatically as fishes and monkeys do, but can walk and move their limbs the way they want to be. Human beings have had a long period of evolutionary development, from the time of the Neanderthal man to this day and probably in the future certain functions may disappear and be overtaken by others (James Owen, 2009). For example, many children currently cannot use the ability to count mentally. They have to have the calculator to go through the mechanism of what they would have ordinarily done a century ago. This phylogenetic development is very important because it tells us what happens from one generation to another in the development of abilities. Children of today are called the Z children, because unlike the previous generation, they can access information through electronic media and arrive at premises, conclusions and assessments, quicker than do the adults of the previous generations. For example, *a Munshi* in a village belonging to the previous generation keeps accurate accounts mentally, but a child of this generation cannot. The child is now dependent upon technology and, therefore, the Z child is known as the technological child. He does not need to go through simple forms of arriving at decisions. He can immediately formulate them from given data. The problem is that if the technology fails or falters, it also confuses the child who is dependent upon it.

The role of epigenesis has been given because we wish also to emphasise that proactive parenting by adults will have to depend upon information sources and media and use less of their own syllogistic powers to arrive at premises. The premises are ready-made and so if the adult wishes to keep up with this era and the fast-moving technology of the forthcoming years, he has to depend upon ready-made formulae which necessarily propel a further intricate set of formulae. The age of the robotic child who is cloned from a biological source is not far away. Therefore, what the parent brings to the parenting situation is his own frame of personal determinants which he may or may not use to affect or influence changes in the young under his or her care.

The setting of the neurons in the brain is according to epigenetic rules of evolutionary maturational processes, where the human brain accumulates increasing cognitive experiences. Over time and space each embryonic process of maturation is on the basis of probabilistic epigenesis, where the next generation of embryos developing into foetuses inherit some of the genetic patterns of the parent phenotype. In common parlance this process is called the inheritance of genes. This is more pronouncedly perceived in the inheritance of physiognomic traits such as characteristics of the young from their parents as facial features, certain typical ways of behaviour, so that, we tend to say, "He behaves just like his father or mother and so on".

The interaction between the adult and their young does not take place in a void environment, namely, devoid of other stimuli. Stimuli surround both the parent and the child and affect their experiences and interactions. The effects depend upon which stimuli are more pronounced, more punishing or more rewarding towards the interacted. The human being tends to move more towards the positive stimuli and avoids negative stimuli. Therefore, on a selective basis, the human being tends to either accept or reject a happening, an event, a situation, that is either positively rewarding or negatively punishing. However, this does not imply that the young are not affected by the negative experiences emotionally and that they do not imprint their mark on the growing younger personality in the interactive process. For example, traumatic experiences in a family such as divorce, quarrelling parents, domestic abuse and, more especially as happens in some traditional families, child abuse affects the child negatively. If a child is constantly scolded, physically slapped or reprimanded or in many cases locked up in a room for some time, these experiences tend to leave their traces on the ontogenetic characteristics of the growing child.

The context of situational determinants also implies the effect of culture, the ecology, and the environmental happenings, which are among the variables affecting the behaviour of the adult and the child. These together with the personal characteristics, which were termed as personal determinants in the previous section, affect the way the parents act and react with the child. For example, if there is an alcoholic husband in the family who comes home late at night drunk and beats up his child, the children watches the terror and confusion and the fear permeates all their other normal characteristics. The children from such families cannot concentrate on their studies, fall into apathy and are, in a sense, "battered". Such external determinants are both known and unknown. The known ones are what happens on a regular basis and are expected. When they are negative there is constant fear. When they are unexpected, there are cues affecting the child in an unknown manner. Sometimes, in fear and some times expected positively. Negative happenings leave the child unable to cope with the situations. Examples are famine, and its consequent hunger, war devastation and such like environmental happenings. When these events are known, both adult and child are in a "reactive mode". In the North-East, for instance, where Maoist movement exists and in the North-West where militants raid areas of Kashmir, these are known and, therefore, these occur in an anticipated basis.

The effects of unknown situational determinants are much more marked, such as a sudden terrorist movement in Delhi, a sudden fire that breaks out in a crowded place or a sudden outbreak of an epidemic disease for which the general public are unprepared. All families and households in a given area are affected by these unknown situtional determinats, more especially the children as the unknown is more fearful to them, than to the adults. In a city, a computer specialist will tend to work even into the night mainly because he is an expert in the technology which is much needed in quantity. Therefore, the more sophisticated the technology, the greater is the ability to expand one's potential skills. Children in these days, for instance, learn to use the computer early and do not have to wait for a chalk and board in the class room to understand or do their assignments. Often because of the availability of the internet, there is no need for institutional learning at higher levels. Students conduct their projects and assignments by plagiarism from the internet and presenting it as their own material and if the teacher is unaware of these sources the student gets away by getting high grades without much effort from his intellectual skills. Similarly, parents unaware of the expansion of electronic media are ignorant of what is happening in the world around them, to the extent that is known to the average high school students. Therefore, skills can be honed on the basis of what is known and if the level of knowledge of children is greater than that of their parents who learned very little of the technology in their days, then an astute child can negotiate so that he has the better end of the stick and is able many times to manipulate the situation to suit his own needs. Therefore, in the last analysis, the interaction between the parent and the child is based on the parental goals and the child's needs. They may not tally. If the child has better skills and greater opportunities than the parent he can in fact turn around the situation to suit his own needs by bypassing the goals of his parents. These situations often occur when the parent wishes to bring up his child hoping he would be a doctor, a lawyer or an engineer, whereas the child is more aware of other opportunities like management of enterprises, advertisement in all its forms, both social and technological, and the availability of many more entrepreneurial and well-paying professions much more than do his parents. Therefore, in the last analysis, it is the question of the growing knowledge of the growing child and the relative *status quo* knowledge of the parent that tend to monitor each other—the child to tone down parental aspirations and the parent to insist on the kinds of aspirations he or she had when they themselves were children. In other words, parents tend to transmit their inherited knowledge onto children without the realization that children themselves are growing independent entities with their own aspirations and needs. This occurs more rapidly as chronological age increases.

Thus, it is meant here that personal determinants, namely characteristics, attitudes and values of the parent generation are important in parenting the child. The child himself in turn is not a clean slate to write on. He is able to understand more and negotiate better through a process of coding and decoding the perceptions of his parents to modulate them to his own way of thinking. Unfortunately, in the Indian context, parents are more traditionally oriented than their children and, therefore, the parents tend to be rigid in their aspirations. Thus, bringing about a disconnect between themselves and the child, parents wish to mould their children according to their own perceptions. In the days of the past, children who were not obedient were punished physically, but now it is well-known that knowledgeable middle class and upwardly moving mobile social class parents know that physical punishment does not bring in desired result and, therefore, tend to verbalize more with their children in order to get them to understand the parental point of view. In certain situations, however, where the parent is autocratic, they do not tend to spend time in explaining why and what for, the parental point of view is more important than that of the child. In the upwardly moving, fast-changing world of families, knowing more and more about the global situations, about modern forms of living, and with better earning than before, parents, some times, in a sense, bribe their children to also move upwards by offering them incentives of cash and rewards or by punishing them by withdrawal of rewards. Neither of these parental stimuli works effectively, for they only tend to cause an inconsistency in their interaction with the child and to, therefore, bring about an inconsistent reaction on the part of the child. By and large, punishment may bring about fear and may for a while suppress the unwanted behaviour, but it often does not get internalized by the child and, therefore, may reappear again and again. The continued use of physical punishment will only cause negative effects on other characteristics of the growing child such as on positivity, the need to achieve and the ability to be emotionally happy and, therefore, in a state of equilibrium.

Thus, we see that the personal characteristics of the parent include what he has inherited from his or her own parents either phylogenetically or in terms of attitudes and values, which he or she brings to bear upon his/her parenting style. These include other personal determinants that are his or her own ontogenetic characteristics. Whether these characteristics are in conformity with the social norms or whether they are in transgression or in confrontation with them or whether they are suppressed, depends upon the individual's differential abilities to cope or otherwise with his or her situational determinants. However, these characteristics are brought to bear in relation to how the parents affect their child in their behaviour, attitudes and values. However, as said before, the child grows up in an environment different from that of his parents and these are not taken into account in the parenting styles used similarly by each individual parent. The probability, therefore, is that all children will be brought up alike, but it is obvious that parents are influenced both by the domains they have inherited, internalized, potentialised and by their ontogenetic or own differential characteristics, which meet up in a differential world of their child who has his own ontogenetic potentials and skills different from that of his parents. How the adjustment between the parent and child does take place in differing parenting styles and in what other respects, in what quality, to what extent, is what makes one parenting style different from another.

These concepts are derived from the theory of reinforcement and conditioning so well propounded by their original theoreticians, namely, Watson (1913) and Skinner (1938 and 1948).

Development of Values and Goals

Development of values in the child is mostly inculcated by the transference of values from the adult care-taker (the adult responsible for the upbringing of the child). A value may be defined as a systematically occurring human disposition attributed to different objects, either concrete or abstract, and priced for the attachment of the individual to the object or the other human being/beings. In many respects, it is akin to a sacred and sanctimonious precious attribute and is usually deep-seated over time. It is also continuous like the value of the child for the mother. More often than not, values are the outcome of the effect of modelling of adult expressed thoughts and expressed behaviour. A value is usually a constant commitment to an idea or an object or a human being. Such valued concepts are esteem, respect, honesty, justice, truthfulness and commitment towards an ideal objective. How does a parent transfer a system of values to the young? This depends upon the motivation of the child to inculcate in his repertoire of responses the ways in which his parents want him to behave. Values can be either negative or positive depending upon whether approved by the society or not. A delinquent, for instance, values a negative behaviour which he/she exhibits in defiance against social norms. On the other hand, most children are brought up to adhere to positive normative behaviour. Values may be categorized as (1) Concepts which cannot be concretized but are abstract like respect, harmony, confidence, esteem and positive achievement, all working towards goal attainment; (2) Concepts which are observed in outward behaviour and are similar to the behaviour of the adults from whom the imitation takes place like, for instance, accepting the fact that all human beings, irrespective of their caste, religious or social class, are to be treated as equal; and (3) Expressed behaviour which arises from the logical construction of the individual child's own thinking in terms of intelligence and cognition such as the thought processes which bring about innovative ideas in any one of the sciences. These indicate a scientific bent of mind.

A value implies a selected behaviour leading to a selected goal deliberately indicated by the adult or logically evolved by the child's mental abilities. For example, if goal attainment is related to achieving a higher reward (either material or non-material), then achievement orientation is valued behaviour in order to attain the reward (the goal). Values do not appear and disappear as temporary. In fact, they are related to needs which motivate the child to want to achieve (values), to obtain a certain level of behaviour/ appreciation/status. Behaviour is not any behaviour but that behaviour which indicates a positive attitude towards a person, place or thing (valued goals). In other words, behaviour is assessed to know whether a person has a value or not. The object, the person or a thing, is viewed as valued if it has worthy merit. For example, we can say that if a child likes to work hard at school, then he has a value for attaining scholastic reward.

There is close communication between the parent and the child. Parents are the foremost source of valued behaviour for the growing up children. The child may also learn to value negative behaviour through the observation of negative behaviour exhibited by the parents, and because he wishes to imitate them, he exhibits the same behaviour indicating appreciation of his negative value. For example, a child may go for shopping with his mother and he observes the mother bargaining loudly and argumentatively with the shopkeeper till she gets her own way. This type of behaviour he learns to imitate as valued behaviour when he himself goes for shopping as he has learned to value this type of behaviour from the parental style of shopping. Thus, the observation of parental behaviour and its repetition by the child tend to reinforce the behaviour in the child. Values, however, do not float in isolation of the network of several other social and economic variables which impinge upon them. A value is learned and, therefore, there has to be some object or person from whom the value emanates. A value, however, is distinctively related to a goal. If, for example, a parent tries to instil in her child the attitude of respect towards others, then she has a goal in her mind, the goal being that the child learns to respect others as a valued trait.

For example, a primary school boy becomes very fond of playing cricket as he has watched his father praising and admiring it and, therefore, wanting to excel in the eyes of his father and liking cricket, he works hard at cricket to gain the admiration of his father which he values highly. Playing good cricket is, therefore, here a channel to gain the appreciation of his father, which appreciation is highly valued by the child. Besides, the child also detects a positivity of admiration of his mother towards his father's achievement at cricket, which then increases his value for the game. That is, he admires the father and, therefore, he tries to learn the same attitudes and values that his father has and directs his actions towards similar types of behaviour as he observes in his father. Further still, such behaviour is reinforced by his mother in him. However, at the same time, there needs to be a felt need as to why the child is disposed towards liking cricket. On the other hand, he may not like cricket at all because he feels he cannot be a successful cricketer and, therefore, is in conflict since he cannot perform the way as wanted by his parents, whose attitude towards his ability is valued. His attitude towards his father's goal of playing good cricket cannot be imitated since he does not have the capacity and, therefore, he desists from imitation.

In a sense they present a model of behaviour which is repeatedly and positively reinforced by the behaviour of the admired adult. This repeated and positive reinforcement inculcates in the child a concept that this behaviour should be valued, which then becomes a core value during the course of his being parented by a caretaking adult or an older sibling, or the biological parent. This need for the child to please the adult, as he is continually being rewarded, which is embedded into his life-space as a value, that is a core value (Lewin, 1936; Lewin, 1951). For instance, the observance of his parent has been honest, and his parent transfers this honest behaviour to the child being parented through positive reinforcement and rewarding behaviour. Honesty, therefore, becomes an embedded value in his interaction with others, irrespective of whether his parent is present or not. It will continue to be transferred to other people in imitation of valued behaviour exhibited by the parent. He will continue to show honest behaviour and disown dishonesty. During the course of his being taught, being guided along a pathway that is perceived by the parenting adult, it being the selected pathway towards goal attainment, he also learns affiliative values which he exhibits in his behaviour in imitation of the adult. This deliberate inculcation by the parenting adult is usually in line with moral and socially approved behaviour. Values usually are morally toned (Kohlberg, 1976). A pattern begins to develop during the course of the child's upbringing and he moves from a valued behaviour to another in his repertoire of interactions with others.

Development of Attitudes Related to Value Systems

The concept of attitudes is abstract and is mainly perceivable in expressed behaviour. This expressed behaviour takes on different tones and is largely in the realm of positive and negative attitudes. Therefore, what is an attitude? An attitude arises from a continuous type of behaviour that repeatedly emanates on cues from the self or the environment. Since this behaviour is perceivable, it necessarily must be related to a perception that is either mental imagery or is related to an object, material or human, in the environment. However, it has to be a feeling towards something in the self or the universe. Attitudes in relation to parenting imply an expression of the self-behaviour arising out of habits. Habits are formed over a period of time and can be negative or positive, as said before, but can have shades of them. In other words, attitudes may be strong or weak in relation with an object or a person. This dimension, positive or negative, has been popularly used in order to measure attitudes using popularly known methods of socio-grams and paper and pencil tests. For example, over time, chronologically speaking, a child develops an attitude of possessiveness towards his biological relations, especially his mother. In a sense, cognitively he gravitates towards the positively reinforcing object and desires to include it within his sphere of perception: sight, touch, taste, hearing and such like sensory feelers. This positive or negative feeling is tuned on when there is a cue from any one of the admired objects in his sphere. If a child sees a fearful dog approaching, his attitude is one which indicates a negative reaction to the dog and, therefore, exhibits a negative attitude towards the object, namely the dog. On the other hand, when a mother reaches out affectionately to the child, she is displaying a positive attitude of love. Therefore, an attitude is not only in relation to an object, arising out of a package of repeated experiences, that form a habit, positive or negative, but is also emotionally tinged. An attitude has to emerge not only out of cognitive perception, but also social cognition as perception is influenced both by the individual's motivation and socio-environmental cues. Translated into examples, we might cite the fact that an Indian child reacts the way he perceives his environment which can be urban, rural or tribal, but more especially the family environment. It is habitual for instance that children learn to revere their parents and grandparents and we often see this happening when youngsters touch the feet of the elders. This is a cultural habit and the behaviour that arises out of it is an attitude. Therefore, an attitude that shows culturally finished patterns is an approved pattern in the given society and relates to its norms. Another interesting illustration is the event that happened in January 2012 when an Indian couple went to a foreign country with their two infants. The child welfare organization in that country used their own cultural norms to assess whether the action of the India parents of force-feeding their children indicated that they were not neglecting their children and after many interviews the two children were taken away to a foster home as the child welfare organization assessed that they were neglected. Apparently, the neglect had to do with the hand-feeding of the children and infants sleeping with their parents are not a cultural norm in the foreign country. In the Indian culture, this is passé, but was anathema to the cultural pattern of the country where the couple had been staying in and where the father was employed. These parents suffered torture till their appeal to the foreign affairs minister in their own country had an effect and within the space of a few days the children were returned to their lawful grandparents in India. The child welfare organization still claimed that the perceived behaviour in their country of these Indian couples was assessed as being neglectful! The grateful parents were happy to return to India to be with their children. This is an extreme example but it goes to show that parents' behaviour towards the child in their upbringing patterns assume styles related to their familial social and cultural environment. The attitudes of parents' practice may be assumed as normal in one culture, but non-normal in another.

How is a habit formed? Experiences that have meaning to the individual, whether adult or child, are usually emotionally tinged. Whenever an adult expresses close bonding in her behaviour towards the child, this expressive behaviour is repeatedly reinforced towards positivity or negativity to become a habit. For example, a child will shrink from an approaching snake, exhibiting negative behaviour, whether the snake will bite or not. On the other hand, the child will approach a friendly dog wagging his tail and try to touch it, believing that this is a positive gesture by the dog. A mother does not question why she loves the child. She usually says in surprise, "but this is an automatic reaction". The term 'automatic' implies a reaction without predetermination, non-hesitant and spontaneous. Repeated such practices form habits. Probably one of the first experiences of a habit formation is when the infant sucks his thumb, and also when he pulls up his feet and sucks his toes. This sucking habit is conceptually a reflex action towards an object. There is no barrier between the perception of the object and the perceiver, namely the individual, who reacts positively or negatively.

An intervening variable is the emotional attachment between the mother and the child which becomes a habit expressed in an attitude towards an object or an individual. Positive attitude is displayed when the child moves towards the source of attraction and reaches out for it or her, and in negative attitude the child moves away or avoids the person or object. Such types of attitudes are always attached to types of behaviour emanating from the individual, pervading perhaps to the whole personality of the individual. Emotionality arises from a sense of perception that is either fearful or joyful. We observe this more clearly when a child cries for his mother and on the first sight of her, his tears dry up, he smiles (emotionality) and reaches out to his mother expressing a positive habit (habit). In sum, therefore, we say that this habitual attitude becomes a part of a habitual pattern of action and reaction to the object by the personality, where the object is either positive or negative. Over time, the behaviour observed frequently becomes a habit and being embedded as a core type of behaviour (Lewin, 1935). On being provoked it reappears and on cuing it, in a sense recalled spontaneously and pervades the human being's action or reaction, either positive or negative. Attitudes form an important variable of parental styles of behaviour. Recognition of the latter depends a great deal upon perceived behaviour of the parent which almost always indicates attitudes. However, the assessing of attitudes needs to take into account the interactive factor of social cognition and, therefore, the occurrence of social stimuli. These occur when there is interaction between and among individuals, especially those in close bonding like the mother and the child. This needs to be further probed to assess the attitudes displayed by either parent or child who in turn is also affected by the environment, both family and social (Holden, 1989).

For example, when a child says "I hate doing homework", he means he has a negative attitude towards homework and this dislike does not change but becomes a habitual pattern of reacting to homework and is displayed by an attitude towards it. In sum, therefore, a habit is an expressed behaviour, repeated over time and accumulating an emotional tone, reacting to the same stimulus almost always similarly on the appearance of the stimulus. Parents as adults like any other individual also develop habitual patterns of behaviour which are expressed attitudinally. A parent who is very demanding towards his child will habitually and as an automatic pattern will keep saying "no" to the child when he wants something which his parent does not wish to give. She will continually say, "No, you cannot have it" and is most likely not to change her habitual pattern in reactionary response to the object—her child. The development of attitudes is a very strong variable in parenting styles and is perhaps very difficult to eradicate or to substitute with another habitual attitude. If one conceives of a bipolar dimension from positivity to negativity, one can always find digression between positivity and negativity. If, for example, a person dislikes another, it can be expressed most of the time, or hardly ever. Thus, attitudes can be strong or weak or even indifferent. When an adult says, I do not care if my child goes to sleep in the afternoon or not, this shows indifference between positivity and negativity in attitude; in other words, a neutral habit. In the development of attitudes, they tend to usually form a relational package. If a person says, I do not like fruits, he means the whole category of fruits, which are something to which he is indifferently disposed. If a person says, "I hate being told what to do", this indicates severity of a reactionary negative habit. That is why, habit formation is very important in the early years of development. Habits are related to the perceived goals of the adult or the child because using Kurt Levin's paradigm these habits are centrifugal, difficult to dislodge and have a course of their own in detailing the personality of a person with strong habits. For strong habits, when consciously expressed, display a sense of high commitment or high intolerance towards an object or thing whether it is a negative habit, or a positive sense of commitment. Concepts like tolerance, compassion, argumentativeness, leisureliness are usually habitual if the person repeatedly expresses the same pattern of behaviour. Habits are more clearly seen in people who say "I have a regimented life" like a solider following a pattern of habitual discipline. These types of adults are regularly set to a biological clock, doing certain things at certain time and in certain places in a systemic way. Any movement away from this pattern dislodges their habitual behaviour pattern.

Habits are, therefore, dependent upon the reinforcement that the individual receives from the environment, whether human or material, as to what he should do repetitively. His mind may be elsewhere, but his conscious performance shows habitual behaviour.

Attitudes are indicators of personality characteristics. If, for instance, a person has a negative attitude towards other religions, he comes to be known as religiously prejudiced (negative attitude). If he has a positive attitude towards all religions, he comes to be known as a person accepting of all religions (positive attitude). In sum, therefore, actions and reactions of individuals, if repeated over time, gets consolidated as repetitive patterns which indicate liking or disliking a particular object, person or thing. Therefore, these habitual patterns become tinged with negative, positive or indifferent emotions/expressions. When a mother goes to pick her child from the school, she has an indifferent attitude towards other children, but when she spots her own child, her attitude is positively tinged towards the child. Then her behaviour demonstrates a love-oriented attitude towards the child. Thus, attitudes develop as a part of the personality attributes in the socialization of the child and evolve mainly from the development niche of the adult's own socialization. She absorbs these attitudes from her parental values, which she then tends to transfer to the interactions with her child. For example, a parent who has had a traumatic childhood tends to deliberately move away from the types of behaviour she had seen in her own parents and adopts an opposite pattern of attitudes.

Values and goals are distinctly conceptual. They are observable either orally expressed by the adult or the child or expressed in the behaviour of the parent towards the child. For example, a parent while visiting her own parents with the child will touch the feet of her parents and gesture towards the child to do the same. This is observed behaviour of a value for respect and if we further extend this concept, it implies teaching the child to learn positive behaviour that agrees to societal norms indicating that the mother has a goal towards which she is directing her child, namely deference towards elders. However, except for the touching of the feet of the grandparents, these ideas or concepts are not revealable. There has to be an attitude in the behaviour indicating respect for elders. Therefore, we see a linkage between the concept of value, its relation towards a goal and its action in terms of expressed attitudes. All these are dormant and are expressed only by the action of the parent of the child by which one can infer that this attitude of respecting elders is valued behaviour.

Psycho-Emotional Influences Affecting the Parenting Process

No human being lives a goalless life, even if it is to live at a primeval level. That the primitive living also calls for the movement of the mind and body, in search of food and water, which are basic needs of human beings, is obvious. The attainment of the basic needs becomes primary goals. This simplistic explanation indicates that there is no homeostasis in the behaviour of the human being unless there is full and complete satisfaction. There is always a movement directed by the mind towards an ideation, whether expressed outwardly or whether internally inherent. The objective may not be attainable, but the quest to achieve the envisualized goal still exists. There is, therefore, a constant thriving to achieve the goal. All objectives move towards positivity in the pathway of avoiding negativity. The objective of the human beings is based on the direction of need-satisfaction. The primitive moves towards water and food, because

(a) the individual needs these items; and
(b) he values these objectives.

Likewise, a child moves towards the desired objects or, to put it in another way, the attainment of the desired objects is his goal because these are necessary for the satisfaction of his needs. This is a simplistic way of explaining the relationship between values, goals, needs and satisfaction of the needs.

A need may be described by expressing its lacunae or feeling the need to fill-up the lacunae. It is when the lacunae exists that we experience a need for plugging that lacunae. The human being constantly seeks what is lacking because of the value or the importance of the object being sought to fill-up the lacunae. However, there is no easy pathway between the need for an object and the attainment of the object, nor is it easy to identify the need when there are several needs demanding fulfilment and competing with each other. An individual lives life for fulfilling those needs which are lacking or are in short supply and is constantly in search of filling up the lacunae till there is a feeling of satisfaction. The individual needs to assess for himself which needs are priority and which are not. In other words, within the complexity of needs, another concept arises, namely the concept of conflict. Conflict arises when there is an equal and competing pull between two or more needs. An individual approaches different desired objects with varying gradients. Generally, the gradient of approach is stronger when the object being approached is more in demand. When there is a striving to attain more than one needs which are experienced at the same time, the human mind is in a state of conflict. As the two conflicting needs race for fulfilment, the one that has greater value for the individual exerts greater pressure in the gradient of approach towards the fulfilment of that need (Krech and Klein, 1952).

Conflict, therefore, is another concept which interferes with need-fulfilment and goal attainment. As such fulfilment can happen at one time in the satisfaction of more than one need. But fulfilment cannot occur at one time to satisfy two opposing needs. The conflict between different needs occurs all the time except at times when the individual is extremely focused only on one goal like running a race towards the goal of reaching a finish-line or writing a test to be finished in time. But, more often than not, there are several demands on the individuals in his everyday life, whether a parent or a child. Therefore, conflict, inconsistency, hesitancy and delays might occur in the goal-attainment, even though some needs might be very high in priority. For example, a sailor whose ship has been wrecked for several days tries all kinds of fishing methods to get fish to eat, but he cannot since the waves are high (barrier), since the sea is wide (no limits in sight), some times calm and some times wild (inconsistency) and, as time goes on, his need (for getting fish to eat) continues to be high and, therefore, fishing continues to be highly valued since it satisfies a primary need, namely, hunger. In this example, the sailor experiences several barriers towards the attainment of the need.

With the above explanation, it is obvious that at any one time, there is a dynamic interaction between needs, values, goal-attainments and the churning of conflicts among the needs. A need can only be observed by either its oral expression or by the gradient of approach of the individual towards the goal.

According to the strength of the need, its expressions vary. For example, a sage might go into a stage of wanting to eat all the time, but because of his spirituality he forces himself to go into stages of starvation in order to prove his need for being a spiritual sage, in avoidance of satisfaction of bodily needs. Perhaps for a while there is a conflict for wanting to eat and not wanting to eat. At times, he might go into a state of moving towards eating the way a natural human being will want to eat, but refrains from doing so by the strength of his need to avoid indulging himself.

Given the socio-psychological network of dynamic and changing concepts, both abstract and concrete, the operation of a rubric is perceivable. If these concepts are put together and viewed from the perspective of one adult, the major perception is that a child should follow these goals in order to become achievement-oriented. The nurtured should not languish into drifting into goal nothingness and aimlessness, irrespective of being directed towards a goal in life by the nurturer. It is assumed that a well-oriented nurturant would be able to direct the nurtured into a pathway of goal-orientation, whether expressed or understood. Goal-lessness is usually not the parents' intention because the behaviour of a child is the reflection of her own inherent values and monitoring techniques used by the nurturer. The nurturer uses monitoring techniques which are continuous in the interaction of the nurturant with the nurtured, so that the nurturant's goals are expressed by the one nurtured, namely the child. Nurturants usually do not wish to have their nurtured aimless and goalless. No nurturant wishes to have it said that his nurtured is aimless or goalless. When children are being nurtured, they are often asked what they would like to be when they are grown up. The usual response is a "a pilot", "a doctor", "an engine driver" or "a scientist", and so on, and, in the case of female children usually "a teacher" or "a nurse". In the case of being asked, there is very little hesitation in replying that they have no aim to be anything. The goals are expressed because these are familiar in their environmental milieu as being highly priced, and they have learned to value these types of professions, which are usually reinforced by the nurturant and hence strongly valued by the adult to reinforce the child's movement or direction towards the attainment of these goals. The nurtured's expression either bodily or verbally may not eventually become evident. Nevertheless, they are always present in the way the nurtured moves in the direction of either expressed by himself or herself or eventually changing in such a way as to be goal-oriented whether it is one goal or another.

They may not become eventually what they say they want to become as their vision keeps widening. But, the point here is that they want to be something or somebody who is admired as they learn from the stories they read or which are expressed by their parents as the valued goals. Therefore, the first goal under all circumstances is that the parent directs the child towards building up a motive to achieve (increasingly given a high motivation, high rewards, high incentive for moving towards the goals expressed by the nurtured or the nurturer). The nurturer also builds up a calm and motivated pathway towards goal-achievement of the goal. However, the goal may vary from time-to-time and the strength of the motivation towards the object may also change from time-to-time. Nevertheless, goal-retention is hardly ever singular or unchangeable, dependent upon the relativity of other motivational factors and also dependent upon the changing environment. It will change according to the influences of other experiences, peers, other adults and the force of the parental motivation and the influencing environment in which the motivated nurturant moves. The third is to value the attainment of the goal, and the fourth is the final attainment of the goal itself, even though the goal might change from one time to another. A girl might say "I want to be a teacher" or "a nurse" or some such caring profession, but more often than not, she is also spurred on to adopt a higher profession as in these days there is very little difference between the goal-attainment of young men and young women. Most of them are similarly oriented towards becoming professional in their movement towards attaining a profession that is of utility to them in later life. By the time, the nurtured reaches the stage of adolescence, he or she pursues the goal with a greater sense of motivated direction. At the stage in which they have to make firm choices as to the direction of the goal, they begin in earnest to be motivated and in working towards the achievement of the goal. Often we observe that many graduates take on specialization courses, like acquiring an MBA, so that they are proficient in the management of their life towards attainment of the goal. This picture might seem a cozy well-packaged one. But the picture of attaining the goal changes from one situation to another, depending upon the strength of motivation and the desire for attainment.

For example, a child's education may be in one geo-ecology when she is a school child, and in another geo-ecology when she goes to college. This is often observed when a child is put into a good boarding school, which has a better standard than the school at the place where the child was living before. A tribal girl works towards the goal of being a good housewife, a good mother and a good human being in the joint family and especially in the occupational work. A tribal boy expects to be proficient in the occupations of his family, whether it is fishing, hunting, arts and crafts of the village or cultivation. The rural parent when she/he is close to urban areas observes many varying professions such as doctors, lawyers, engineers, and such like, and he or she, therefore, aspires that his/her child also becomes a doctor, a lawyer or an engineer. The stronger the attraction to these new-found goals, the higher the motivation to attain the goal—either mentally or physically, or both. These goals which we now term aspirations, because as the higher up socio-economic ladder or closer to occupation to the urban ecology that they are, where she sees these occupations, they become more goal-oriented and their motivation to achieve becomes stronger. Thus, we see that there is a tribal boy or girl is circumscribed in their rise from the rural to the urban and within the urban parameters, climbs up to the social ladder to attain a higher profession and so inspired by the environment he climbs as fast as he can. However, all these concepts assume that the child is flexible and directed towards the parental goals and aspirations for him or her, but in actual fact, this may not be so. We have known of altercations between parent and child in the parent prodding the child to do what the parent desires and the resistance of the child towards parentally prodded careers.

When all these concepts are together, namely achievement-orientation, the focus and the direction of the child to move in the pathway reinforced by the nurturer, the value of the object of the person as a goal and lastly, the attainment of the goal itself, they form a package from which several other priorities fission out, and ultimately settle on the one which has the highest motivation in the rubric of the goals that circulate around the nurtured. For being achievement-oriented, there has to be inculcated in the child a need to achieve (Murray, 1938; McClelland, 1961).

There has to be in the child a compliance with the aspirations of the parent in a focused manner towards the objective indicated by the nurturer, towards which there is continued reinforcement. Therefore, the motivation requires to be continually reinforced. There has to be a pursued motivation that is undeterred towards the goal and finally, there has to be the attainment of the goal in spite of barriers like shortage of money or having to take evening classes while working or some such limitations. It is because of the motivation that the children are urged by the adults' persuasion to continue to move along the specified direction given by the parent.

The Psycho-social Dynamics Influencing Parenting Styles

The major schematic pattern of behaviour is well-known to be stimulus response pattern of behaviour which triggers connecting thoughts/behaviour in the nurtured child. Such thoughts/behaviour enlarge the experiences of the child as he or she goes through his/her life phases. The adult nurturing the child has gone a long way accumulating such nurturing experiences for the child, to which the child acts or reacts positively or negatively. The undertone of these experiences is the emotionality of both the nurturing adult and the responding child. There is still much to be said about the interacting dynamics between the nurturant parent/care-taker and the child, depending upon their own personality dynamics. The adult may have grown up in an aura of being authoritarian or democratic or *laissez faire* depending upon the impact of the experiences that they both the parent and the child accumulates in their range of experiences, while the child being care for is developing these characteristics and gets embedded firmly in any one of these styles, which is used more often as a marked identity of the child.

There are specific psychological theories from which these characteristics spring. Most of them are based upon the Dynamic Stimulus Response Theory (SR Theory), or the Topological Theory of Lewin. Social Learning Theory emphasizes environment, namely different geo-ecological areas in which people live, learn, work and try to fulfil their aspirations. The social learning theory emphasizes the observation and imitation of others in the "micro" (family) and "meso" (neighbourhood, school and such like) systems. The individual is encouraged or reinforced by his caretakers to imitate models. Mostly the parents become the models for their growing up children.

According to Stimulus-Response Theory, in the socialization process, children are reared towards perceived goals of the parents. They learn by imitation from an adult. During the growing up the child learns deference towards elders and values such as politeness and amicability. If the parents reinforce diverging characteristics of positive behaviour, such characteristics are eventually inherent in the behaviour imitated by the child, which becomes part of his personality (Bandura, 1977). If the child shows an interest in learning a particular behaviour and is constantly being reinforced in that behaviour, the child develops a need for achievement in the direction of the goal envisualised by the adult, stimulating the child in that direction.

These theories refer to the influences on the personality of the outside world, moving from the innermost circle of the family to the outermost circle, or the macro system encompassing the entire world. As vertical and horizontal mobility occurs in the social realm as the child grows and matures, the child comes in contact with members of his peer group, the neighbourhood, the marketplace and other areas of events. He learns about the global world through social media and might visit various places thereby gaining a world vision. However, the theory of Kurt Lewin also vividly amplify about the mental phenomena of active and creative thought processes which occupy various regions of the mind, some becoming centrifugal, others becoming centripetal, the latter influences changing their position from time-to-time as growing experiences relate to them. However, the centripetal or the core values learnt from early childhood continue to remain with the individual as part of the child's personality throughout his life except when overriding intervening variables change even the core values. The Theory of Cognition is the basis of the social learning process and implies cognition, recognition and decognition.

The Theory of the Unconscious

The unconscious is embedded in the mind, is deep-seated and difficult to recall into the consciousness. All individuals differ from each other even to the minutest detail in behaviour, in thought, in action and reaction to personality variables and others and ecological aura surrounding the caretaker and the child. What is observed in behaviour is the outward demonstration of the inner workings of the mind. The one aspect the most observable is interpreted as outer workings of this inner self. According to Kakar (Sudhir Kakar, 2012) unconscious operating in the mind of the adult during the process of interaction with the child is important. In this context, it must be emphasized that in studying the unconscious layer of action and interaction between the mother/caretaker and the child, the mother/caretaker is rarely understood. In fact, there are little information on the workings of the inner mind (the unconscious) interacting with the child. In the western world, much is known about the unconscious, especially in the context of teaching and learning and unable to fathom why they act the way they do as they have little knowledge of the unconscious.

Little is known about the operation of the unconscious to the average mind. In the context of parenting, since there is little knowledge to the average persons as to how the unconscious operates, all that they know is that something inside the mind is bothering them and they do not know how to tackle the situation and so they move from one set of operations to another without really examining the inner layer of the working of the mind.

Much of this outward expression is also to be seen in different endeavours on the path of the observers to perceive this outward behaviour in a selective manner. More often than not, the perceptions emanating from the observer's need not necessarily coincide in a simultaneous manner. The expression of the inner mind is also selectively perceived. The commonest forms of these differential perceptions are toned by the need arising from the observer to perceive only those aspects which need not express the behaviour expressed by the observed. In a familiar fashion, this is often observed when there are tangential need motivation between the perceived outsider and the expressed outward behaviour of the individual so observed.

However, the same ideation may be expressed in a form that is not understandable by the perceiver, like for instance, expressing the ideation in a language idiomatically or otherwise in such a manner that is to put it mildly as "erratic behaviour, "irony" and "sarcastic" in even those expressed by the behaviour (physically or mentally) in such a manner that further confuses the perceiver.

Perception is, therefore, dependent upon the need of the observer, the type and amount of language used by the individual's need ability and, therefore, the transference of the idea in its clearest form. Indeed, oral language is by and large the most skilful method used by those individuals who express only that part of behaviour which would cause the perceiver to either make clear the action or thought or which confuse the observer. Often we hear the term "what I mean to say is this and not that" implying the pathway selected by the individual's performance. These expressions might be exhibited in a positive or a negative manner or perhaps more dubious in a "double tongued" expression emanating from the one attempting to explain what he wishes to say either clearly or dubiously understood by the perceiver.

Thus, the adult, when fully grown as a parent, has a combination of need-reduction, social learning and is affected by the environment around him which then constantly changes his attitudes and possibly his values. Most often, values change when deep-seated experiences which have a traumatic effect occur and, therefore, evoke unconscious thoughts which had been buried in the past, but which, however, unconsciously continue to influence the behaviour of the adult towards others and especially in the parenting process towards the child.

Such being the case over the years of growth into adulthood, the parent is influenced by what he has observed from his society, namely, societal norms and behaviour related to it. The parent also learns that the parent should fulfil the basic need of both herself and her child. For example, as the female adult was growing, she learned in her primary school years what is right and wrong, morally and socially from her own parents, especially her mother. Most of the time, this is verbally expressed by the mother. Sometimes she learns it through body language and at the same time it can be either positively or negatively reinforced behaviour. Perhaps, as a child she may have been physically punished, when she was caught being dishonest and she had to suffer the humiliation of being scolded by her mother in the presence of the other siblings and thereby shamed, which continues to stay with her a long time as behaviour to be ashamed of (social learning). The times that she was positively reinforced were very few and so she grew up harbouring this negativism about physical punishment due to children who transgress societal norms.

Further, her parents were great readers and travellers and some times, she would go with them on their travels. So, she came to know about events outside her family circle. There were times when in the company of her peers, she was often pushed aside. She, therefore, sought all the means possible to be in their company.

These are, therefore, some of the major characteristics of the individual who eventually from childhood becomes a parent and who, therefore, will use his/her own childhood experiences in the upbringing of the child. It might just so happen that if these are deep seated needs and negative then she will tend to eschew them in her parenting tasks. If they have been positive and pleasant, then she tends to repeat them in her parenting style. Then again, because in her childhood, she might have accumulated a great deal of knowledge about other countries and other cultures she might make it a point to teach her child about these countries, their customs and social mores. This concept is termed the transference of characteristics of the adult to the child and could consist of a host of cultural ideas.

When the parent brings up a child there are several barriers she herself has to meet with. They arise from her own needs and motivation, from the needs of the child and from barriers in the environment, both known and unknown, whether she succumbs to them or not depends on her strength of mind and will and often if compelled by other priorities she may even submit to these barriers giving rise to a sense of self-incompetence and frustration. Thus, the child might then experience a host of inconsistent perception from the adult caretaker. These attitudes of consistence and inconsistency happen routinely as no one individual is perfect in following a perceived pathway all the time. They change from some perceived needs to another. Intervening variables may be either from other situations which rise along with the parent and many times, a sense of conflict and, therefore, guilt and conflict are two of the most eroding barriers in the parenting pattern of interaction with the child. A mother, for example, might strike a child, then feel guilty and follows a sense of conflict as to whether to make up with the child or to still continue punishing the child or to forget the punishment and begin to act normally. These dynamic perceptions and actions interact in all forms of parent-child interactions where conflict and guilt are the most pervasive. The least consciously aware is the parent about these uneasy feelings, unless she takes time to introspect and understand why she is upset and why her child is not behaving the way she would want him to. All that she is aware of is that she is uneasy and unhappy about what has happened. This punishment of the child has well been described by Sears, Maccoby and Lewin in their explanation of the kinds of techniques that parents use. This is called the physical techniques of child rearing *vis-à-vis* the love oriented techniques, the latter being a kin to the egalitarian-*cum*-democratic pattern of parenting (Sears, Maccoby and Levin, 1957).

Besides this type of interaction that criss-cross dynamically and change from time-to-time, depending upon the cues from the parent or the child, a whole dimension of experience builds up which can be retrieved when occurring again either by the parent or the child. It is essential to mention here that the same parent may not deal with child the same way that she does with other siblings in the family. There is a unique relationship between each interaction and action of the parent with each of the children. Further still, the parent is at all times consumed with her set of needs towards other members in the family when dealing with one or the other of the children in the family. Therefore, the interaction with any one child in the family is always influenced by other intervening factors such as the mother may have just had a quarrel with the husband and the effect of it is added to her reaction to her child, or she might have heard some bad news or even so she may have heard some happy news and may be very leisurely oriented towards interaction with the child. Thus, in the interaction process with the child, the following nexus exists. The need of the mother's interaction with the need of the child, the power of the mother in relation to the powerlessness of the child, the continuity or discontinuity in the mother's attitude towards the child, the lack of instilling a sense of values and lastly the lack of clear goals in the interaction process.

Given these juxtapositions of conceptual frames within the mother, within the child and the action and the reaction processes is the all-pervading dominance of the personality of the mother as we have briefly described above. Therefore, how do we arrive at a conclusion that there is a pattern in the processes of communication and interaction between the mother and child?

Where the parent has set for herself a pathway towards determining her child's behaviour as being one which will happen, she will logically and in a persuasive manner interact in such a way that the behaviour is explainable for the child's basic understanding that it is for his good. This involves treating the child as a compatible human being to whom if explanations are given that are amenable to reason or where he is rewarded by love-oriented techniques and physical punishment is aborted, he will learn that this is the socially acceptable way in which there can be an equilibrium between himself and his parent.

The Negotiating Child

Given a high cue grasp, some children learn to be astute negotiators. They learn from cues in their parents' non-verbal behaviour and body language what to expect and what the reactions would be if they did not comply with the instructions or the guidance communicated to them by the adult. They learn to circumvent punishment and act according to the adult's expressed goals. They might become indifferent in their need-achievement and in their goal-orientation. Many parents do not think that their parenting techniques which evolve into a parenting style is an important influence on how the child behaves and over time what kind of an adult she or he would eventually become. The concept of social imitation and learning is extremely important here whereby the mother learns that parenting is a serious influence on the child's personality even though it is not consciously exhibited. The relationship between a parent and a child is well-known to be one of close bonding, arising from the symbiosis since conception. To the child, the caring mother is the most important figure in his or her constellation of interactive adults.

4
Parenting Processes Affecting the Development of the Young

The parents set a paradigm of needs, motivations, directional behàviour for the child. These have varied strengths, and are set in a purposeful way by the adult, stressing the direction the child should take, and emphasizing the goal to be attained. The child is reinforced constantly and more frequently in the direction emphasized by the parent. This pathway has been expressively propelled by the need to achieve. The paradigm is circumscribed by needs, motivation, reinforcement and the constant guidance by the adult towards setting the child along the pathway perceived by the adult caretaker. Within this paradigm, there is either compliance or conflict on the part of the child, who is either negatively reinforced or positively reinforced.

There are as mentioned above several person-directed or environment-directed cues emanating from the parent and from the child himself. There has been attempt here to emphasise the pathway perceived by the parent and the persuasive prodding of the parent in the direction towards the goals as perceived by the parent. This purposive behaviour, propelled by the parent, need-directed. The parent may not be persistent in this direction. She/he may vacillate from one style to another. In other words, the parent may be inconsistent. The child, therefore, bewildered by the lack of need-expressed behaviour, either emphasizing the child's own needs or reinforcing the parental ideal type of behaviour.

The term parenting implies a process. This process is a unique relationship between the parent(s) and the child. This process is common to all born creatures, whether mammalian, aquatic or otherwise. The parenting process implies a continuation of the relationship between the biological young and the old where there is a nexus or tie between the child and the parent. The process of parenting consists of a combination of behaviours, feelings and expectations that are unique to a particular parent-child relationship, the relationship being biological bond between the parent and the child. During the parenting process a unique dimensional bond develops between the parent and the child. In nature, it is the older of the species that exert influence over the younger. In this influencing scenario, those influenced are affected on the basis of the unique characteristics of the older person, where the older influences the bond between the older and the younger.

No interactive process in a family is like any other in terms of the type of bonding. For example, a mother may have many children, but her bonding with each child is differentially characterized. Why do we call the adult-child interaction a process? It is because the relational effect is influenced by the differential personalities of the differential older person or parent who has the social right to influence or has social-psychological power to influence the younger. Even though there are many children, each bond is different from the other. They are differentially tinged. For example, a mother might have more than one son and more than one daughter. She could interact differentially with the older son in a more mature manner than she would interact with the younger son. Each interaction has its own specific motivation emanating from the adult caretaker or the parent or from the child's own need to achieve and, therefore, the mental make-up of the child, who proceed along the directional path laid down by the parent or his own pathway. The two pathways might interact positively and become a consistent, constant reinforcement. There might be inconsistencies. The adult does not always perceive the same directional pathway, but of changes from time-to-time. The parent may even be casual in his interaction most of the time, or the child is less likely to be influenced by parental direction. This interactive pattern influences the needs of the child to overcome the directional pathway set by the parent. Similarly, the mother would treat the older daughter in a more strict fashion than she would treat the younger daughter. Each parent-child bonding is not without its own unique emotionality. There is a love-relationship between the older towards the younger, which is caring, and which is protective in its context, when compared with the bond with another child. The parent takes care of the feeding, looking after the health, the education and the development process of the young under the parenting umbrella of experiences.

These differential experiences arise out of the characteristics of the parental figure, where no one parent is like another. In other words, not only is parenting a continuum but it is also a special symbiotic emotional relationship with another human being in the process of cooperative upbringing.

The above is written in an abstract format only in order to reinforce the fact that parenting is common to all creatures and is a continuum, with a differential in that the interactive process with each child in a family is dealt with differently by the adult parent. If we operationalize the above abstract theoretical concepts into everyday life, it implies the following:

> The female adult has within herself the internal or inherent capacity to care for the young children. She nurtures them and are often called nurturers or caretakers.
>
> The primary nurturer provides the basic essentials towards the development of the younger.

Nurturance implies that each nurturant mother uses strategies in caring for the child differentially from any other nurturing mother. She does so using different methodologies, that brings about equanimity. For example, identical twins, although from the same chromosome as the other, behave and act differentially from each other as the same mother uses differential techniques in the upbringing of children even when they are twin.

The process of bringing up a child is not a smooth process, nor is it a process that can be predicted at any one time. Each stimulus differs from the nurturing mother to the child in varying situations. The nurturing processes of interaction are differentially applicable as there are different types of nurturants, by age, sex and temperament. Therefore, each parent is differentially cued when interacting with a different child.

Beyond a certain point, when the child is fully matured, the nurturing process has no effect as the process tends to be similar. When the nurtured attains adolescence and puberty, he/she is likely to break away from the nurturer and the child uses his own independent thinking and traits without the influence of the nurturant. There is likely to be some altercation between the nurturer and the nurtured as the nurtured grows older, differentiating capacities to develop in certain way different from another nurturant in the group of children and the nurturant and between the children of the same family and the nurturants within the family fold. This movement from dependency to independency of the child implies the beginning of adulthood of the child where he or she uses his/her own ontogenetic traits and skills to create further experiences for himself/herself leading to independent decision-making. The whole process of this continuum from birth to independence is termed parenting.

Sources of Trait Development in the Individual

How does a human being become a grown up individual from birth onwards? As chronological age increases, physiological development increases. The female develops a feminine figure which not only affects her physiognomy, but also attitudes and goals whereby she uses her techniques to reach these goals. She can no longer behave like a tom boy; climb a tree and go to watch boxing matches, as society spearheaded by the parents mould her into such feminine ways which imply female roles, culturally attuned. Fortunately, parents themselves have gone through this process of cultural acculturation, so they are aware of what is required of them in the nurturing process. Therefore, it is a cyclic repetitive process from one generation to another, where role-behaviour and values are reinforced. The parent brings up a child using certain strategies that are knowledgeable to her/him, attempting to monitor the growth and development of her/his progeny according to the societal norms of the culture in which the individual lives. The child, in turn, simultaneously develops his own traits, weaving into those that are nurtured and monitored by the parent, but that originate ontogenetically, which branches off into different directions. This is akin to the way of a full grown tree develops its branches, each branch moving away in different directions. In the same way, each child in a family behaves and makes its own independent ways. What is the source of these traits that are chronologically and maturationally developed? Looking at development through a genetic perspective, epigenetic rules set the parameters of the individual's development. This is done through a developmentally progressive process in which the individual's development takes place because of his or her inherent ontogenetic propensities. As said before, his own genetic processes mature in individual contexts, some faster than the other, some multi-dimensional and other a little slower. That one is certainly not like the other.

This is observable in young children who do not like the same things as do their parents. At times, they will deviate somewhat from their parents' behaviour, attitudes and even values. This heterogeneity in behaviour between the biological parent and the child is also observable in children of the same parents. For instance, in children who shirk strangers, in children who are friendly with strangers, in children who love animals, in children who are afraid of them, in children who are timid, in children who are aggressive and daredevils. Yet all originate from the same genetic map or genealogical mapping. One can go on adding to this list of differential traits, some of which are said to be inherited, some of which are said to be developed by the individual or by the nurturant's insistence on certain traits being stronger than the other. These ontogenetic traits can be potentialized or depressed depending upon positive or negative reinforcement of the environment, especially, the human environment and mainly that of the cues emanating from the nurturant.

There has been much debate on whether intelligent traits have been inherited or is ontogenetically specified. We do, of course, often hear of perceptions of similarity in traits such as the daughter is like the father, or the granddaughter has inherited the grandfather's eyes. It is not impossible that a dominant or a recessive gene works to create these characteristics in the child or grandchild, but more often than not, as a child grows to become a young adult, differences are very marked in terms of the heterogeneity of psychological characteristics though not as heterogeneous as in physiological characteristics. For example, one can immediately distinguish a south Indian from Tamil Nadu as totally different from a Kashmiri from the North in which the physiognomic make-up is differential.

The Influence of the Dominant Characteristics of the Personality of the Parent in the Parenting Process

All human beings, as they grow from being infants (of their parents) to be matured adults, eventually develop their own personality differentials, even if they are twins. In other words, as they grow they also develop certain repeated behaviours which together contours a personality, each different from another. The meaning of a personality is that it is organized behaviour accumulated through experiences and over time and hence leads to the development of a personality. Eysenck perceives the organization of repeated behaviour patterns which become the personality of the person through habitual responses and reactions to experiences in the world around him.

Hall, Lindsey and Campbell in their description of personality lay emphasis on the integrative or organizational function of personality, implying that personality is an integration of discrete responses of the individual in a synchronized pattern (Hall, Lindsey and Campbell, 1998).

The uniqueness in the description of what the personality is both a socio-psychological one combined with a bio-organismic one. This conceptualization takes into account the perceiver and the perceived, the perceiver being the human world around individual which characterizes the personality as being aggressive, submissive, confident or lacking in confidence and such like qualitative characteristics which denote how the individual is perceived both by others and internally perceived by himself/herself. To perceive these characteristics, however, the individual, i.e. the perceived person, has to indicate this amalgam of characteristics which make up the amalgam of inherent traits which propel him or her to be aggressive, to be submissive and such like, to portray some major characteristics more than others. This is like, for instance, a boy showing aggressiveness in behaviour which he has nurtured within himself and which is more frequently observed than either regressiveness or mildness. The personality has to operate in an environment where she or he can be identified. That is why when we talk about parents as personalities, we identify the parent as being aggressive, submissive or even as not exhibiting any dominant characteristics which are observable. When we say that a person has a pleasing personality, we imply that the person is good-natured, is compatible and is a person with whom a rapport can be established. In other words, it is easy to get along with that type of personality. Words are mere qualifying descriptions. But they take on meaning when attached to individual who can be identified as being mostly aggressive, mostly regressive, or mostly pleasant or unpleasant and such like. In the context of this book, we do not fission out into so many descriptive additives, as they then nullify the predominant or priority characteristics in the making of a personality. Therefore, if an individual exhibits predominantly certain bio-social characteristics, she or he is identified by the additive describing the composite organisation of that behaviour which appears dominantly in the child growing up into an adult. This dominant characteristic is similar to being autocratic or where implicit behaviour is expected of the child, limits are provided and any violation by the child is strictly regimented. On the other hand, when an individual accumulates during childhood characteristic behaviour which shows meekness, mildness and submissive behaviour and does not confront the child when he or she misbehaves, we tend to call this type of a parent a casual parent with indifferent behaviour towards the child regarding compliance or otherwise with the parenting demands, instructions and such like. On the other hand, if the parent shows a conciliatory nature, a willingness to explain what is expected of the child and why the child should behave in a certain way, the parent is indicating a planned nature which is willing to compromise and, therefore, to deal with the parenting process democratically or on an equal basis. Over the decades, during the Elizabethan period in Europe and still in some countries today, parenting was dominating. The child was to be seen but not heard. The child was to comply or to take punishment and child was to follow a regimented and systematic type of behaviour. Later on, the democratic way of interaction was prescribed as being more achievement-oriented and, therefore, by positive stimulus and positive reinforcement the child was persuaded to behaviour as indicated by the parent. Further still, there are societies where children are left to their own devices except when they overstep certain limits which are socially non-acceptable when violated. Generally speaking, therefore, the three forms of styles of parenting may be identified, but that is only in a pristine form. The intervening variables affecting the parenting styles are:

(1) Ecology,
(2) The Psycho-social dynamics of parenting,
(3) Socio-religious beliefs,
(4) Socio-economic class, and
(5) Ecological influences.

(1) Ecology: The relationship between man and nature is bound by the surroundings that each have with each other and the outcomes of these relationships that man has with nature is indexed by the term 'habitat'. The habitat of any man is the natural surroundings and the interaction of man with his habitat. Bringing this relationship down to simplified words, it means how man interacts with his habitat consisting of others with whom he lives. The individual lives with his biological parents, other relatives spread out into interacting with the values, attitudes and with the circumstantial events around him on an everyday basis and in consistency with repetition of the same type of action and reaction to various stimuli in the environment. The first interaction is with the biological parents and siblings. As the individual grows a multitude of relationships develop and multiple interactions become complex. It then becomes essential that he maintains an equilibrium all the time between himself and the multiplicity of interactions in which he has to set priorities and operate on them. The child's interactions become more and more complex and bewildering as he begins to go out of the close family circles and enter into the school stage. He feels the need to know which interaction should be given more priority and which should be given less priority. For example, if the English language for a high-schooler is easier to deal with *vis-à-vis* mathematics, he will tend to spend more time on the latter. As he grows older, the attention he pays to mathematics becomes more complex and more difficult to deal with. He, therefore, seeks more assistance with which his parents may not be able to comply with and, therefore, he requires a tutor in order to raise his competence in the area of mathematics.

The individual child as he grows chronologically becomes more demanding and demand more prioritizing. Therefore, the child moves away from the first ecological base, namely the parental and biological sphere, which comprises his first surroundings or his first ecology, which forms his micro-system. His second ecology is his meso-ecology which explanatorily implies his relatives, friends and neighbours as he widens his spheres of interaction. This meso-system means a wider interaction with many new spheres of activity for him.

As, for instance, the school, the market place, and the neighbourhood—which further expands into wider geo-ecological areas, which then have wider implications for interaction. The interactions in this system are based on the necessity of interacting on a differential basis every time that the children meet with differential experiences. At one time, he might be attending an event such as a school function, at another he might be going on a trip or meeting with the people. Then comes the outer world of which the individual is totally unaware, namely the world of which he happened to have had an idea only from Television Channels. According to Bronfenbrenner, these are interactions which grow in a widening system of interaction to which the individual is exposed. His first exposure is to the micro-system, namely, his family; the next is to the meso-system; followed by the *exo* and macro-systems of interaction or of knowledge. A school child may come to know of the world around him as he grows chronologically older and as he is able to gain information and/or interact with others on a widening sphere.

The Various Types of Parenthood

In a normal family, there are usually, both mother and father as parents and in a joint family system, them are other relatives in addition to the parents. These relatives often act towards the child in compromising their technique of parenting in order that there is equilibrium. It becomes necessary to examine how the husband and wife relationship influences or monitor the way the child behaves and in what ways the mother acts in her role as a parent in contrast to the male parent. As is well-known in India, most families are patriarchal in their structure, and the wife often follows the patriarchal system of interaction with family members. It is often that the mother is influenced by the child-rearing patterns that her own mother knew and transfers the same ideologically to the progeny. Girls are brought up in a feminine way, while boys are brought up in a masculine way. Thus, the trend is also influenced by the kind of child-rearing pattern of caretaking that is used in her childhood and she unconsciously transfers it to her own children. The mother has mentally itemized the kinds of behaviour of the child as influenced by the parenting behaviour, which her parents used with her and she unconsciously transfers it to her own caretaking pattern.

There are still other situations, where the parent is single and has to depend upon her own knowledge and experiences, and those from the media and friends which she can use in her parenting practices to guide and monitor her child. Single parents, especially those with one child, completely interweave their own knowledge with those of friends or relatives and social media so that she is constantly modifying her behaviour towards the child. Thus, it is to be observed that parenting patterns are influenced by those around the parents who are relational or are in a friendship pattern with the mother, advising her in her caretaking roles. This rubric of interaction with relatives, friends, media brings to bear upon her utilization of that which is comfortable with and transfers into action in her own parenting styles.

Yet again, there are children who are orphans and have no care-taking adult. Further still, a child may be relegated to an institution where there is very little emotional care and mainly directions of behaviour. Usually, in the latter situation, behaviour is controlled by negative reinforcement, that is, non-verbal, negativism or even physical punishment with little explanation as to why the institutional caretakers treat the child the way they do like any other child in the institution without the foundation of love and protection and belongingness towards the child. Frequently, caretakers in institutions keep changing and, therefore, the child is exposed to many different styles or patterns of upbringing as influenced by these various adults around the child.

Therefore, not only do we have the case of the parental figure using a parental style evolved from their own inherent trait or as influenced by environment, and as learned from childhood, that there are various combinations of caretaking patterns. Super and Harkness (1986) identify the milieu of child-caring as consisting of (1) the physical and social settings in which the child lives; (2) the customs of child care and child rearing (in the specific culture or sub-culture of the child); and (3) the psychology of the caretakers. They call this process "the developmental niche". The phylogenetic and ontogenetic traits are interactive and may vary in different time. This interactivity depends upon which genetic trait is the more predominant at any given time when the parent is dependent mostly on her ontogenetic traits in guiding or directing the child. In other words, these are characteristics which are her own inherent traits. They are not those that seem to be like others, they are known to be individualistic. We have in this documentation concentrated on the last, namely the ontogeny of the parent and have indicated that the parent follows customs and societal mores of the particular society/community in which the parent lives, which indicates the physical and social characteristic of the parent and the child in interactive mode and also as influenced by demographic and geo-ecological variables (Khalakdina, 2012). This latter concept, namely, physical and social settings, are emphasized by Bronfenbrenner in his identifying a micro eco-system, namely the family and other adults of the household and the customs and conventions of those in the particular ecology in which the social settings occur and might change from time-to-time. For example, if the father of the household is working in a Government job and is transferred from one city to another, then the child is in upheaval, moving from one city to another, and perhaps a new sub-culture, such as a Gujarati child moving with the family and go to Tamil Nadu. Then, issues like finding schools for the children, finding a suitable dwelling and knowing where the market places are, what the costs of living and such like details become an additional chore for the parent, disrupting the previous pattern of caretaking.

The presence of either one of the parents influences the child's behaviour since they are more or less constantly present with the child. There is also a process of socialization in which the parents modifies and monitors the behaviour of the child.

The physical setting, namely the ecology, the social setting, namely, the culture requires a maintenance process which the parents follow. They build up an environment for their child. This is contributed to by their own processes of monitoring and moulding.

India has several climatic and geographical conditions which affect lifestyles and, therefore, pre-dominating patterns of behaviour. For instance, in the Northern Hills, where climate is cold and bleak, the inhabitants have to adjust to their habitat. In some parts, cold for the most part of the year like the upper Himalayas, people live a very stoic life for survival as the climate is difficult and the terrain is also difficult to modify. There is need for stoicism which parent uses in a systemic mode. This sense of stoicism is highly ingrained in the upbringing process. In this instils a hardy character in the child or children case, the parent (Minakshi Chaudhry, 1998).

On the other hand, living in a metropolis like Bombay or Delhi exposes the growing adult to a world of increasing social media, electronic devices and technology. These are all fast-paced instrumentations of the world around. The adult living in a metropolis is exposed to a fast-moving pace of time and technology. The adult, therefore, incorporates the experiences with these items of the existing and predictive technological world, automatically and thereby has a style of communication that has a higher level of technology than the adults living in inadequate meagre ecologies. Modern technology, therefore, includes teaching the child how to learn to use the computer, the mobile or to understand signs and symbols and to be attuned in such a way that competition requires building up a high achievement in mastering the environment both created by the human being and the physical world of climate, geography, demography and offers the adult a pathway to progressiveness, which the adults may or may not adapt to. More often than not, the parenting style adopted is to use the world of technology as a teaching aid towards goal direction, which the child needs in a competitive and highly professional milieu, especially amongst the middle and upper classes.

Therefore, the tendency for the modernized parents to use an egalitarian pattern of communication, persuasion and instilling a high need for achievement in the child is apparent. On the other hand, if we move to a rural area, time is of little consequence except as determined by the seasonal changes which affect agriculture and so the world of the ruralite is attached to agriculture and the rural or the tribal economy. Therefore, in the rural environment there is a tendency where everything is attuned to seasonal changes and the nature of the economy. These environments dictate the vagaries to which the individual human being has to adapt to. The tendency of the parent is to be less harsh with the child as time is not limited and interaction can proceed leisurely. It is very rare that the life of the tribal, the rural, and the urban crisscross each other except for those ruralites who knowingly go to urban areas to seek jobs. Nevertheless, these migrants do not have a permanent ecology in the urban areas since they are in a migratory pattern of living. They often go back to visit their families in the place of their origin. This pattern is most observable in the life of the domestic workers who take time off to visit their original habitats, which keep the family network more or less intact.

Nevertheless, whatever may be the ambience in which the parent operates, the fact remains that not all parents live a normal life with a happy husband-wife relationship, both agreeing to bring up the child in the same parental style without much differences. This is perhaps because they deal with the same environmental habitat to which the child is attuned. In practical reality, we feel that the ecological setting, especially the human, has much to do in influencing the parenting styles.

Intervening and Extraneous Variables in the Caretaking Pattern or Style used by Parents

We now move to the specificity of the actual operational situation that the Indian parent finds herself to be in. As is well-known, an individual, parent or otherwise, lives in a specific region (ecology), with a specific habitat surrounding the parent (environment, both human and material) (and surrounded by a similarity of the ethos, to which the community is attuned), such as a tribal or rural or urban setting with other adults as in a joint family setting or with relatives and friends in close proximity, or is single parent and manages on his or her own. We indicate that then extraneous variables are the social media, the ideology of the culture, the caste and class of the parent, and ethnicity/religion of the parent. All these extraneous factors operate to influence the styles of parenting.

Geo-ecologically, a tribal parent, for example, lives in a close habitat in a region that is deeply forested or inaccessible hilly tracts, living with her tribe, following a routine of customs and conventions which is transferred from one generation to another, with modifications as dictated by humans in the environmental ecology. The parent's living style is a hutment in the village or *Jhuggi* in the city, and probably, as in some tribes, she lives in a polygamous family with "other wives" and the sense of security is kept together by strings of loyalty and attachment and an isolation from cosmopolitan areas. Therefore, it is reasonable to assume that the parents imitate the patterns of parenting styles which has been transferred from generation to generation. Further, if the parent has been exposed to a different environment than did her forefathers, he or she is less likely to be imitative of their patterns. She would either try to preserve the parenting pattern used by her own parents or would try to modify to create an equilibrative environment. Or, if highly educated, will change in terms of modernity that she is faced with, using knowledge obtained from books, from teachers, from *Gurus* and such like social and educational media. These new sources of information tend to replace the models she has inherited from her parental environment. She follows the style of parenting used by her parents and everybody else where the child is everybody's child such as in joint families in the rural and tribal areas. Therefore, whatever her parenting style, whether dominating or equalitarian or *laissez faire*, it is strongly influenced or perhaps greatly eroded by other adults around mother who often act as mother surrogates. Therefore, to identify parenting style would not be difficult as it would be mainly generic in these specific geo-ecological tribal areas. The more urban, the setting in which the mother operates, more information temp to influence her to behave like the parents around her in that setting.

Given the fact that India has the largest rural population, 750 million, sustainability of development is of significance. Since, the rural and tribal livelihood depends upon the produce of land, the demand for lands by the industrialists is at the risk of dislodgement and deprivation of the lands of the tribals. This is a very potential threat considering that the urban parameters are increasing in terms of geo-ecological behaviour, according to the mode in which the community is living. Thus, even when we say the tribal lives a sheltered life in decades to come, it is not going to be so, simply because of the invasion of urbanites demanding more and more of their property and often times dispossessing them at very low rates of exchange.

For human development to be sustainable, the locale of the parent and the child should continue to be the same for familiar communication in the same environment, in a familiar language at familiar places. In the last century and growing at a fast pace in this century, family members are being dislodged rapidly as urbanization creeps in. To take a simple example, the construction of buildings in the urban areas requires casual labour. Because of off-farm services being low, ruralites and tribals leave their places of origin in search of livelihood in urban areas not only causing a surfeit in the urban areas of poverty-stricken people, but also causing a dislocation in the parenting process. This might sound far-fetched, but in social reality, for example, parents who work on construction sites leave their young children with NGOs, while both male and female parents work, as in the structure and systems used by mobile crèches when they move with the newly employed construction workers in helping them [illegible]k after their children (Khalakdina, 1998). As soon as the j[illegible]ne place is done, the contractor takes them to another pl[illegible]work and so on. This disruption, therefore, does not giv[illegible]ssary time for parent-child interaction and, therefore, for the prevalence of a systematic style of parenting. If the child is not with NGOs, then the older siblings act as mother surrogates. This disruption, therefore, does not bode well for identifying a particular parenting style.

Dr. Abdul Kalam uses the word 'PURA' (Providing Urban Amenities in Rural Areas) for sustainable development (Abdul Kalam and Sujan Pal Singh, 2011). For this reason, if rural and tribal migrants are to lead a wholesome life with just as many amenities as the locals do, then it is possible to talk about their sustainable development, whereby they will have the kind of amenities that the inhabitants have or as specified by Dr. Abdul Kalam, providing urban facilities in rural areas would be a solution for retaining the migrating rural and tribal families in their own homesteads to improve their own livelihood and, therefore, have a homogeneous parent-child interaction process, thus leading to the identification of the parenting patterns or styles. Since these haphazard demographic changes will continue as providing amenities for the rural and the tribal has not occurred since the last 60 years, it is but logical that these rural and tribal families will be drawn to amenities of the urban areas. Therefore, the kinds of parenting styles in shifting geo-ecological areas are likely to be mixed from without identification of definitive parenting patterns. But like the shifting sands of the deserts, the environment of the tribal is constantly being exposed to change. This does not mean that the whole families move from one ecology to another *en masse*. We might hazard a guess that probably the most prominent style would be the *laissez faire* type since neither of the parents have time for child care. By contrast, a well-settled middle and upper socio-economic classes in urban areas also gyrate towards not only having mechanical abilities in their home environment, but have recourse to informed centres of parenting such as social media, television, education and such like newer information technologies as time goes on. There is likelihood that perhaps out of the two socio-economic classes, it is the middle socio-economic class that will provide identifiable parenting styles. In the upper socio-economic classes, there is the likelihood of there being a mixture of egalitarian and *laissez faire* parenting style. Where the parenting adult is with the child for most of the time, the interactional activities will cumulate towards providing a parenting profile which is likely to be egalitarian, as not only are there the necessary amenities for a livelihood, but there is also time to spare for the mother-child interaction processes. In those sections of the middle socio-economic group who are educated and value the need for a large amount of experience for their children, like going with them to watch their matches, to take them swimming, to introduce them to new scenarios, the likelihood of a democratic *aura* prevailing may be much more portended than in the case of upper elite. In this group, parents are both working at top speed from morning to evening and hardly see their children and one might guess that these children are looked after mainly by housemaids. Therefore, the pattern of parenting in elite group is usually that of the housemaid who takes care of the child and the major activities of the parents is to overindulge them, because they suffer a modicum of guilt that they cannot and do not spend their time in parenting, and when on holidays, take them to expensive sites and bring them back, patting themselves on their backs that they have done a good job of parenting without the realization that the children do not need a quantity of items to keep them busy, but quality time of parents who need to spend time with them to understand and act according to their aspirations, their attitudes, their values and their goals towards life. As the children from the upper class families grow-up and go away, they tend to become highly independent and in a kind of aggressive manner seek from their parents more and more unconsciously substituting items of consumption for parental time, interaction, love and caring.

The tendency is that the world of the rural is more circumscribed, has less experiences to communicate to the offspring with and, therefore, often the full potential of the offspring is not tapped. With the urban elite, the tendency is at the other end of the dimension and in real fact; these children know much more than their parents and can in fact teach them a thing or two which the parents do not know. Thus, parenting styles are haphazard, non-identifiable and where interactions are *at the moment for the moment*. Thus, constancy and continuity is not likely to be identifiable as any one such type since the situations, both personal as well as material, change from time-to-time, with little tendency towards regularity of interaction and caring for expressions. This is not to say that parents of the upper elite do not care for their children. It is just that other priorities overreach and takes over the actual time for interaction, in transferring goals, values and aspirations.

The Influence of Caste and Religion on Personality Outcomes

Perhaps there is no country like India where caste is a system affecting the lives of people. In spite of this being the second century of freedom from the colonialism of the British, caste still continues to retain its basic parameters of distinguishing between and among the castes. Caste as a very strong factor has been acknowledged and several treaties have been written on it. It is what one is born with that is one's *Karma* and during the process of this incarnation the entity or the *jiva* has the option to either progress in *adharma* (evil deeds) or in *dharm*a (good deeds) which then account for the next *avatar* or the next rebirth. This is a strong belief no matter what the additions and subtractions may be. In other words, the fissioning into the different sub-castes again into which one is born and cannot change. The different castes operationally define the major occupational tasks that are necessary to carry on as being a member of the community into which the individual is born and brought up as a member of his or her caste. It is the lower castes who occupy the lower rungs of occupations like sweeping, cleaning and such like unclean or 'lowly' occupations. The Brahmin, is the caste most esteemed. It stands to reason that being born into a Brahmin caste the individual is exposed to many personal, religious and family prohibitions and prescriptions within that sub-caste. When attached to religion, there is a variety of pantheology of godheads and adopting one or the other as the house god, as for instance, the Radha Swami group uses Krishnaji as the symbol of God and in most sub-castes in the south, Shiva is the Godhead. This does not mean any one form is discredited, but that all these forms spring from the same Godhead and if closely allied castes live together, there is very little stigma, but if a Brahmin is living next to a "lower" caste, it is considered prohibitive to interact with him, especially in terms of food, according to the ancient scriptures. For, there is a hierarchical acceptance of which caste can mix with which caste and except for the lowest all the others are allowed to interact with each other, namely, the *Harijans* (the name given to the lower castes by Gandhiji). Of these, the Brahmin is important because it is essential that only he can perform the religious rites during marriages, births, *pujas*, ritual ceremonies and such like.

How does caste, therefore, affect parenting? From early childhood, it is the parents' bounden duty to expose the child to the meaning of God, to expose the child to the meaning of good and evil and to identify the Godhead of the household as their guiding spirit. There is wide acceptance that any household may use any Godhead, because of the belief that all Godheads lie in the only one, the *Paramatma*. In this way, there is an easy coalition among the castes except those who perform menial tasks like the *"Harijans"*. Over time, this term has been negated and is now reclassified as the Scheduled Castes and there are other low castes, which are known as Other Backward Classes (OBCs), implying that these castes have not been given the facilities of the upper castes. Caste is an important factor in relation to marriages, in relation to occupations, and other aspects of life. However, as time goes on these distinguishing caste differences are being coalesced in order for communities to admit that caste is a man-made terminology and does not really distinguish between one community and another as being caste bound. One has only to look at advertisements for marriages, to know that this is an essential feature of marriage alliances. Different castes have their own Godheads and perform their own ceremonies, always under the guidance of a *Pandit* or a Brahmin. Notwithstanding what the philosophy of the Government is in relation to the treatment of the lower castes, the parents of the other castes strictly follow the injunction of caste rituals that have come down to them from their own parenting styles. The most rigid of these ritualistic practices are marriages into one's own caste (endogamy), but not one's own *gotra* (exogamy). The parent in the initial stages usually begins with moral education as to what is right and what is wrong. She tells stories about the lives of the Godheads so as to make them familiar and likeable such as the stories of the *Mahabharata* and *Panchatantra* with the reinforcement being positive and regular about the Hindu religion. The child follows rigidly what is said and does not question. The same may be said about children being raised in other religions where religion is an initial and strong streak of the line one must follow to live according to the socio-religious norms. However, no other religion has the caste system so vividly portrayed as in the Hinduism. It, therefore, limits the parenting style to inculcate in childhood the various folklores and myths that are related to the various Godheads. Such folklore stories are narrated to inculcate positive behaviour in the child, and to inculcate morality and ethics in the child's lifestyle.

There are various other religions in India which are allowed to flourish at their own pace such as Christianity, Buddhism, Jainism and Islam. They are classified as minorities and are given special protection. For instance, the Vaishnavas follow the teachings of Vishnu, while Ganesh is the God of good fortune. It is left to each family to follow their own traditional Godheads that had come down through their household lineage. As such, a mother from Bengal in her parenting style might give illustrations of the Goddess Durga. The Radha Swamis use the softer version of the God, namely Radha Krishna. In all this, Ravan is eschewed by all religious sects as he is the bringer of ill-fate. Thus, a Brahmin parent in her parenting style and through her household behaviour will induct the child to the Brahminic way of life and in the maturing and growing aspects will continue to degrade the lower castes, namely, the *Harijans* because they are considered *achhuta* (Untouchable) and the Brahmin as the Brahma or the ultimate in the caste system. In India, caste is, therefore, a highly volatile variable and, therefore, merging into one's caste is considered highly desirable.

Thus, in general rubric of individuals living together and yet professing their own religion, a sense of togetherness prevails, unless of course, there is deliberate fissioning from one religion to another and suing these differences as separatism, which generally does not prevail as more and more adherence is being given to treating all alike and in fact giving special protection to the minority groups. While the older generation are quite firm on retaining their inherited socio-religious values, the younger generation with their exposure to the modern world seem to be moving out of this regimental cycle of marriage within caste and certainly not within close relatives as is practiced in certain southern parts of India (Levine, 2008). Although if religious marriage is to take place, then all aspects of the good of the Godhead bestowing blessings will be incorporated into religious system. Even to the minutest details of rituals when there is a break-away from the parental Godhead, the world of cosmopolitan crosses globally often times. Marrying into another religion is not valued, although increasingly we often find inter-caste, inter-religious, inter-racial marriages taking place all over the world, especially in highly cosmopolitan cities like Bombay. However, there are places in India where consanguineal marriages take place as some times happens in South India and in some tribes.

In the parenting style, therefore, caste and religion play a significant role in the transference of value systems, as children are usually made to attend these religious ceremonies throughout their chronological age. Through the peaceful years the child is accustomed to the norms of caste and religion transferred from the parent. But, when independence begins during adulthood, the child usually makes his own choice as to whether he is a very caste-bound individual or whether he can move from one religion to another with ease. The latter usually occurs when children move in cosmopolitan crowds as and when they go to Western countries for study or work.

Therefore, whether autocratic or *laissez faire* or democratic in parenting styles and in the aspirations of wishing their grown up children to marry their own kind, this often times causes a break-away when the needs of the children become alien to the needs of the parents. It happens more often when the parents themselves are from two different caste groups or two different racial groups.

The Influence of Culture and Socio-Economic Class in the Parenting Styles

Indians belong to diverse sub-cultures as they are divided along the differences in caste and ethnicity, race and religion, ecological regions and languages. In view of these differences, Indians as a whole cannot be said to be subscribing to a unified set of customs and beliefs about child-rearing practices. The major influential factors on child-rearing practices such as socio-economic status, education of the parents and their individual experiences combine with these aspects of cultural differences in determining the contours of parenting practices of each individual parent belonging to the different sub-cultures.

In spite of the sub-cultural differences, India being predominantly a Hindu country, Hindu beliefs play a large part in the child rearing practices in India. There is a general belief among Indians that the children are capable of learning from a very young age and that they must be given guidance to inculcate the values of obedience to authority, passivity, and interdependence. Childhood is viewed as a sensitive time period where children are mouldable. Thus, the parents are believed to play an important role in child development along with other environment of the child. Indian mothers enjoy much physical closeness to their babies. They often carry them close to their bodies and breastfeeding is the norm. Many Indian mothers massage their babies daily using either oil or *ghee*. Co-sleeping during the early years is another characteristic of the close mother-infant relationship. Indian mothers tend to be strict in disciplining their children, who are taught to obey their parents. Scolding, yelling, slapping, and spanking are considered appropriate and necessary for socializing children. Some mothers feel that beating should be used to punish the most severe offenses. A study published by the *"Journal of Paediatric Psychology"* showed that physical punishment is more prevalent in India than in the US.

Indian families show preference for male over female children. A female child is often seen as a financial drain on a family. In addition to paying for her living expenses, the girl's family must pay for her wedding and also dowry, but after she is married all her future income goes to her new family. As a consequence, boys are relatively more well-fed than the girls, and the former receive better education and health care.

India is predominantly a Hindu culture. Its customs, coming from the past age one being preserved and followed so as to guard the traditional ethos of the family. That is, it is traditional in its orientation towards the past and future life and the *atma* is believed to be continuous from one life to another. A mix between and among the regions and a mix between and among religious groups causes a fair spattering of interaction in and among various cultural groups, and therefore, there are many sub-etioses, and there is much respect between one ethic group and another, where communities have their own sub-religions, typical socio-cultural practices and traditional ways of behaviour, mainly exercised by social class and social wealth.

It is well-known that 70 per cent of the Indian population live in poor regions where there are mostly agriculturists living on the vagaries of changing fortunes in terms of income and livelihood means. There is little cultivated land, where terrains are hard to access and where people in fact stay bound to their natural ecology. The main overriding factor in the life of the people here is day-to-day economic activities for earning a livelihood. Parenting in these ecologies is a struggle to provide the parented child with the essential necessities for a fairly decent livelihood in the initial years. That is why the major reason for school drop-out is that the child has to help out in family occupations and household tasks, if at all male children are allowed to study further since, they have to be the major wage-earners. In these circumstances, it is a usual societal norm that a fishermen's child along the south coast dresses in a *dhoti*, goes barefoot, learn to catch fish and live in shacks. A Himachali, at the other end, has to wear warm clothes to keep away from the cold winter/winters, lives on meat, which has high proteins, and since the land is fertile and fruits and vegetables are pretty available, he has a normal life where he is not deprived of the essentials for living. In fact, if one were to minutely examine the ecologies in which different communities live, it is easy to see that it is not too difficult for different communities like fishermen, huntsmen, agriculturalists, shepherds to live in an ecology to which they are accustomed for their livelihood.

Again, a child in Mumbai does not have to think twice about whether he is well-clad or not. He goes to school and if the equilibrium between himself and his family is steady, he tends to be need-achievement oriented and, therefore, is prodded to be a professional by the parenting style used by his parent(s), as the parents are usually reinforcing towards professions for their male children.

The different parenting styles discussed above in the previous chapters have been found to apply across cultures and socio-economic classes. But, research has also shown differences in specific parenting practices such as that in all cultures parents with lower socio-economic status are more likely to use 'authoritarian' parenting styles than those in higher socio-economic status groups (Hoff *et al.*, 2002). However, the positive effects of authoritative parenting differ across cultures (Dornbusch *et al.*, 1987; Deater-Deckard *et al.*, 2003; see also Phoenix and Husain, 2007) in some degree or the other.

It is, therefore, well-known that even though there are three well-known and high-profiled styles of parenting, these may be low grade or high grade depending upon the supportiveness of such factors as geo-ecology, psychological make-up of the parenting adult and the parented child and the cushioning of such extraneous variables like caste, religion, ethnicity and socio-economic status etc.

Culture encompasses a totality of the way of living in the composite of all these factors in a given ecological space. For example, the culture of the Pangis in the Himalayan upper hills is different from fishermen along the coast of Malabar, yet their culture is by and large Indian. The differences and variances occur in minute styles. They vary from one parental group to another depending upon the ideology of the family, especially of the caretaker in the upbringing of the child in the family. If there is harmony in the family, then the frequently occurring parenting style will tend to prevail without being shaken at its roots. However, if there are contradictions and confrontations among the members of the family (in the caretaking processes), especially between the husband and wife (who are the parents of the children), or mother-in-law and daughter-in-law (who live in the same household), then the stability of any one parenting style is shaken and can only be used, if not opposed, by the other adults in the family who also have the power to guide, direct and monitor the child's behaviour. In fact, when there is acrimony in the presence of the child between the mother and the father, the likelihood of inconsistency in parenting will tend to prevail and, therefore, debilitate the child's behaviour. Children in such circumstances may fail to abide by the guidance of the mother or the father, depending on which one of them is the major caretaker, which may differ from family to family in a given community. The child may, therefore, grow-up with using a confused lifestyle with differing practices only because these have been reinforced by the major caretaker on the child. When his parents make up the very changeable nature in the practices they use, either being very strict in one ideology, changing from one to another, the confused child does not exhibit a lifestyle that is harmonious with the rest of the family, or with either the mother or the father. When there are sharp quarrels, castigations of infidelity, the child being parented loses his faith in the guidance and aspirations that his parents motivate him towards.

The above concepts are illustrated in the paradigm below:

Table 4.1 : Household Paradigm: Ranking of Positivity to Negativity

Positivity	*Parenting Situation*	*Positive or Negative Situations*	*Probable consequence in the child*
↓	1. Two parents	Harmony	Harmonious continues behaviour.
		Conflicting communication	Inconsequential behaviour.
	2. Grandparents—no clear roles as it becomes a multi-mix of differences in guidance	Supportive of parents	
		Overlaying communication affording the child opportunities for taking advantage and under-cutting parenting communication.	The clarity of the ideology. Wavering. Consistent throughout. Indifferent response.
Negativity ↓	3. In-laws—the probability of argument, confusion	Non-interference	
		Interference and offering opportunities for diversions for the child using different escape mechanisms.	
	4. Extra familial relatives	Supercilious agreement	
		Bonding and relatively with other members of the family living in the same micro eco-system and exo and meso system	
	5. Step-parents or other relatives	Indifference, uncaring and frequently negative in response to the child's demands	Indifferent, stubborn, non-compliant and irresponsible behaviour
	6. Divorced parents	Restricted quarrelling in presence of child	
		Lack of the care of anyone of the parent	
	7. Orphaned children	Bland life	
		Loneliness	
	8. Hostel	Intermittent support	
		Lack of personal maternal care	
	9. Single mother	Totality of both at any time leading from overprotection, spoiling, punishing and regimentation	
	10. Adopted Parents	Creating dependency and meticulous care	
		Uncaring and casualness	

The above tabular formation moving from positive to negative can also be reversed, which means that at any one time, positive or negative interactions may prevail. Interventions and reprimands may occur moving from positive to negative in a uni-dimensional fashion. In the above Table, there is no specification of any one style, for it speaks of different individuals who occupy the role of the caretaker and each one of these positive or negative indications applies in general to any one of these different individuals—adult or children—depending upon the kind of personality traits. It follows that the adult personality traits are much more firmly ingrained while the child will show vacillating behaviours since the child is learning to adjust to the vagaries of personality traits of the adults surrounding him/her, and, at the same time, learning to formulate his own. We have deliberately used these different individuals highlighting their positive or their negative interactions with the child only in order to indicate that, in a given household where parenting goes on, it need not be restricted to only the biological parents. Each one of these individuals has some type of relationships with the child and, therefore, the right to interact with the child is accepted by the actual parent, either negatively or positively, and, therefore, in a kind of elastic manner, they indicate a kind of interactions or activities which are profound, deep, repeated and continuous, which might be high-profiled in any one of the typical parental styles: autocratic, democratic, *laissez faire,* and movement from one to the other at different times, depending upon the strength of each of these ideologies and the persistence of the parenting individual. Take, for example, the orphaned child. It is not difficult to posit that this child is ruled over by several surrogate mothers who have different styles of interaction with the child. In the case of separated parents, the child tends to format his behaviour according to the one parent who is stronger of the two and who modifies the child's behaviour in such a way that is easy to follow. Their arguments and quarrels do not give him any focus and instead they vacillate from one end of the dimension to the other of caring or non-caring, being over kind to being uncaring, dependent upon how the relationships are structured between divorced parents. How often the child moves from parental umbrella to another and what causes a sense of belongingness or does not cause a sense of belongingness depends upon which parent he is more attracted towards in following instructions or in the willingness to follow the modification by the parents as he is more attracted to one parent rather than the other parent.

Similarly, one can hypothesize about the relationships with other members of the family who might take up the dominant role in nurturing. This configuration assumes that all these individuals have some relationship to the child being parented, either biological or through some other affiliations like adoption, surrogate mothers and such like situations, all within a household regime. Given a household of people where there are parents and children, and other adults who are relatives, parenting can happen between an adult and a child, but in interaction with others who are related, both biologically and by law (and any other affiliation) and occupying/moving in the same household area (where interaction is possible), even if temporarily like members meeting together for a marriage or a festival, there is bound to be much weight about the bringing up of children. Those who have authoritarian styles will speak the loudest and those who do not have these high-resonant styles, will speak less about how children should be brought up. It is but natural that the more closely the parents live with their children, the more centralized is the interaction. However, as children grow-up in maturity and independence, they also have lessened ties with the parental figure, since they have formulated their own personalities according to their needs, and, therefore, in the household situation, they are on the fringes of the activities that take place within the household. Adolescent children, for instance, use their homes, mainly for eating, sleeping, working on their computers, and rushing off to school or college where they are more inter-mixed with the peer group and, therefore, adhere more to the values of the peer groups. As they grow old into and beyond adolescence, they tend to formulate their own independent personality-driven behaviour. The younger the children, the more centralized are they with their parents. The more older they grow, the more offstage and centripetal are they with their parents, and the more centrifugal are their personality.

The configuration of the individual parents and their children given above in the paradigm must be viewed from the point of view that this is a dynamic paradigm changing its configuration from time-to-time in response to personal and situational determinants, as indicated in this chapter above. For any one individual can change and become another type, operating in a different set of ideologies and again reverse to an original ideology which is more predominant. For example, if a child loses both parents, the grandmother might take over the parental goal, offering the child perhaps much more love-oriented techniques than even in the case of parents. From the above, therefore, we can specify four very important concepts:

(1) The development of the personality of the parent as a child, brought up by her own family;
(2) The strength of dependence *versus* independence between the parent and the child;
(3) The overload of demand of love and attention from the child; and
(4) the growing maturity of the child to form his or her own identities.

These variables interact to create lows and highs in the interactive processes between the nurturants and the nurtured. These interactions can be culled from the day-to-day activities between the parent and the child.

5

The Consequences on the Child of the Three Predominant Parenting Styles

Before expanding this chapter, it is essential to note that underlying all human behaviours are three parts of the human personality which, according to Sigmund Freud, are the Id, Ego and the Super Ego. While, the ego is considered the executive of the total personality, it always remains subservient to the wishes of the Id, which is the strongest of the three parts of the personality throughout one's life. The super ego is that mechanism of the mind which consciously directs the individual to work in consonance with the approved activities of the society. The three levels of consciousness relate to each other in a dynamic manner and can be compared to the way in which the mind works almost in a three layer manner. The ego is the conscious self; completely aware of the various factors of the knowing of what is going on in the mind and where and why. The super ego is akin to the relationship between the morality and spiritualism of the mind as compared to the happenings that are taking place mentally and are interacting with the mind in a dynamic manner, overseeing the happenings of the mind that relates to the ethics of the thought processes and purity of action and interaction. The id, which is the lowest level of interaction, is unknown to the knowing mind of the individual and its activities take place in an unconscious and unknown level. Every human being, whatever the age, has these three layers of activity, either occurring singularly or in interaction, and further interacting in a confused manner. The ego is in complete command of activities. Whereas the id is the unconscious processes operating in such a manner that the self is unaware of the known morality of the basis of thoughts and activities that go on in the mind without the self having no command. The cognitive map of the individual, at whatever age, is composed of an ego, which is both conscious and unconscious. The unconscious ego is not outwardly obvious, but works within the capacity of the super ego of the individual (Freud, 1935).

The genetic inheritance and ontogenetic tendencies influence the born child (Fuller, 1960). As the child grows in collecting experiences, influenced by the nurturing process, he finds focus. The development does not stop with physical growth but continues by accumulating psychological and social experiences throughout the life span, by which the individual forms an identity and inter-personal person (Burkitt, 1992).

Inner self-depends upon the impact of experiences occurring in such a manner which influences the adult and the child. The activities of the child occur in such a manner that they do not effectually represent the total happenings in the mind that are approved by the society at large, but occur as influenced by the id.

Some of the child's experiences during the nurturing process are stored in the unconscious and are expressed as the need arises in a conscious manner. For example, if the nurturing parent feels that the nurtured child is behaving in a stubborn manner and refuses to listen to the commands of the nurturer, the nurturer may use punishing techniques to control the behaviour of the child. The child often times resists the directions of the nurturer. The child may consciously comply with the directions of the nurturer, but he also suppresses his initial reactions to the nurturer's direction into the unconscious. The nature of the child, therefore, is like a kaleidoscope, acting and reacting to the changing personality traits of the nurturer as expressed and perceived along the needs driven by the inner self and reinterpreted by the self to suit the occasion over which the individual needs to have command.

These aspects differ from one human to another because of the heterogeneity in the ontogenetic make-up of the individuals. Besides the same human being, whether adult or child, can change his or her behaviour, as dictated by the circumscribing personal and situational determinants. Each and every individual is not a Robinson Crusoe. The human make-up is such that he lives as a member of a group, large or small, sophisticated or less responsive to given cues either by the environment or by the commanding and demanding adults in the environment which affect his thinking and behaviour. These encircling sets of variables, either personal or situational, tend to influence the growing child, and during this process the child is internally directed to build up an identity (Erickson, 1977). The identity is formed by the genetic and ontogenetic traits within the human self.

Given these directional pathways the combination and the inter-combination is quite different from that of the child being taking care of to that of the caretaker or the parent. Each individual, therefore, is differentially attuned to influences of other personalities and other situations. One child may have totally appeasing personality while another may be a rebellious personality, while a third may have an indifferent relation to others around the child as well as those around the parent-caretaker. If there is a child who has a timid reaction to the attitudes of the parent who is dominating the child, he would more likely follow the well-defined pathway of the parental caretaker. On the other hand, a child is more likely to be rebellious to parental commands if the parent is less resilient. Again, it is possible that the child may be reacting casually to the pathways indicated by the parent.

Cohesiveness exists when there is harmony between the caretaker and the child. When there is dissonance there is more likely to be differences in attitudes, values and goals between the child and the adult. Where there is disjointedness as, for instance, between democratically leaning child in relation to an authoritarian parent, the dissonance between them may be sharp in the interactions between them. Again, where the child may be indifferent to following commands and is less likely to follow parental pathways, there is less likelihood of harmony between the parent and the child.

It is during the stage of adolescence that the childhood comes to an end and the growing individual develops his own personality and identity in the circumscribed group in which the child lives (Erickson, 1977). Within that group, it is his biological family that attempts to shape him according to the values and attitudes prevalent in the family environment. Since the adult female nurturer is the main caretaker in influencing the development of the child, using techniques that relates to a particular ideology, the child in being pliant or receptive to the cues emanating from the major nurturer and thus tends to follow the directions of the nurturer. Therefore, the influence of the nurturer is the major directional pivot which the child tends to follow in order to please the nurturer and to contribute to the harmony among the members of the micro group, namely, the family in which the child lives. The child lives in the family as a personality different from others in the family group, as he is moulded either by the love-oriented techniques used by the parents or by the negatively oriented practices in the child upbringing. These influences, as we have said in Chapter 2, arise from attitudes, values, aspirations and goals which form the nexus of the totality of the influences that the parent tries to influence the child to follow the patterns set by the nurturer. By these patterns, the nurturer thus influences patterns of behaviour, gets the nurtured child to be motivated to follow the behaviour engendered by the nurturer. Being the pivot of the kaleidoscope of variables affecting the major directions towards which the child is influenced, the child tends to build an ego that identify him as an entity different from others so that he is modulated by the influences of others around him. The nurturer herself is directed by her own aspirations for the child, which envelops the child. The child, however, is not a chalkboard. The child accepts and rejects that which does or does not meet his needs and his own envisualised goals. Therefore, to speak about a one-time pattern that makes up the ideology is not predictable, for any kind of normal behaviour does not go on endlessly and unchanged.

There are little falls and little rises, namely, inconsistencies in the interactive holistic pattern. Therefore, it is essential to not only emphasize parenting styles *per se* but also to find out what the reactive patterns which the nurtured child follows as cued in by the nurturer. If the child is brought up in a tribal family, it tends to behave like the members of the family in which he lives and wherein the families of the communities adhere to in terms of socio-economic, ethnic, socio-religious and the moral values of the community/family in which he lives.

This process of development hinges on the nexus of communication (verbal or non-verbal), interaction and other influences. The child's understanding in the earlier years of growth is more plastic to influence than the influences that affect him as he grows up chronologically, when he develops his own identity formulated according to his own needs and aspirations. As he shapes his own entity, he absorbs types of behaviour advocated by the parent or rejects those which do not fit into his paradigm of need fulfilment and goals. He is in a sense developing his own identity and, therefore, grows away from the parenting style that is brought to bear upon him by his nurturer and builds up his own significant image which he presents to the micro and macro environment of human beings he lives with.

Children also have built-in image of themselves in the ways of thinking and behaving. In the adolescent years, it is more probable that the child is more apt to listen to and behave like the members of his own peer group and, therefore, is more likely to steer away from the ways in which the adult caretaker tries to influence the child. There are various ways and means by which children, as they grow into adolescence and young adults, assume their own styles of interaction with the actors of the family and friends to develop their own personality in the growing up process. The aim is to achieve independence. Therefore, the child selects a mode of behaviour which is attractive, appealing and self-directed.

An Adult parent attempts to transfer to the growing and maturing child, through a set of activities, the kind of behaviour they wish the child to adopt, according to their own perceptions. Therefore, it is necessary to specify the kinds of reactive behaviour that becomes permanent in the child's development as he attempts to move towards young adulthood and to be come an independent adult. These set of activities are attached to each other as they are repetitive patterns of interactions occurring everyday. All children have to eat, bathe, sleep, dress and go to school as all children have to go through modicum of everyday phylogenetic behaviour. Their sphere of activity moves away from the biological parents, through the biological siblings, through the peer group, into the unknown world at which time the child should develop his own identity. At this time also the child achieves a focal point of close interaction in the family from where he moves in the directions which he is motivated to and follows the pathway he needs and aspires for. These activities are similar for all children, but what makes for a paradigm of a trend that is pivotal, that is fundamental, that is focused and high-profiled, is the parental style which takes from all these activities and gives to all these activities a certain attitude, a certain tone, a certain manner in dealing with each situation.

An authoritarian parent might say to the child, it is time for you to go to sleep; and an egalitarian minded parent might persuade the child to get to sleep, using manner and tone and persuasion that more or less meets with the child's level of motivation. A *laissez faire* parent, on the other hand, might say passively to the child, "I think it is time you went to bed". The three diametrically different directions create a corpus of activity which differ one from the other in different directions.

1. Compliance or egalitarianism,
2. Regressive or *laissez faire,* and
3. Aggressive or authoritarian.

How does one instil a sense of responsibility in attitudes and values of the children they nurture, in any one type of parenting ideology used as styles by the nurturing adult. Responsible types of activities are generally imbued by the nurturant in the child so that the child is influenced by responsive and responsible parenthood influences. Thus, it is obvious that at one and the same time, the child grows up in such a fashion that he mixes his own needs and aspirations with those of his nurturant parents. It is to be remembered that this interaction occurs in an environment which is conductive or not conducive to how the child perceives his pathway should be. There may be barriers at some places in some modes of interaction, which the child either has to overcome or interact in such a manner that there is appeasement and a manner in which he disposes of the negativity. The type of consequences repetitively exhibited by the child is a mixture of his own needs which he goes through either in a confused manner or he finds a level of appeasement which leads to harmony in behaviour with the expected behaviour of the nurturant. Therefore, what are the consequences of this interactive systemic pattern of interaction with the nurturant and the other important members of the family that may or may not impel the child to follow a certain pathway or not. In the previous pages, it has been pointed out that the nurturant is an adult and the nurtured, the child, biological or adopted or fostered, within which circumferences the child grows in a chronological pathway. It has also been indicated that this pathway is impelled by either the parent nurturant being authoritarian or egalitarian or *laissez faire,* and in these processes either singularly positive or singularly negative, the child follows a pathway of behaviour either singularly or intermixed among themselves so that either the child is confused identity or finds a singular pathway where there is singularity or mixtures of different types of ideologies thereby causing a confused pattern of behaviour exhibited by the child. Much of the type of behaviour exhibited by the child which is singularly one pattern, as for instance the child exhibiting the authoritative influence of the parent or a democratic reaction to the type of behaviour exhibited by the nurturant, which is singularly democratic or singularly casual, is dependent also upon the consequences of the child's behaviour to these types of parental behaviour, so that eventually the child grows up to be authoritative or democratic or *laissez faire*, whereby the child behaviour can be recognized to be one that is a follow-up of demands, commands and authoritarianism influenced by the parental behaviour, whereby the child listens and adheres to modes of behaviour whether the child is expected to be in consonance with the expected behaviour, i.e., preponderantly demanding and following parental commands, invariably so that the parent is conscious that the child is following a repetitive pattern advocated by the nurturant's directions.

In the same measure where the parent's ways of behaviour influence the child's behaviour such that the child has a democratic interaction with the parenting directions and yet there are other situations where the child is oblivious to parental directions and where the child tends to react irresponsibly to parental directions and follows them in a casual manner. Yet, at the same time, it is not to be forgotten that these three patterns are interactive and while there might be a preponderance of one type, like, for instance, authoritarianism or democratic or *laissez faire*, there is tendency for these patterns to change over a period of time. There is yet a major nurturing goal which is to influence the child more or less in one way, rather than any another, namely authoritarian, democratic and *laissez faire*, and if there is a relativity of adherence of the child to the nurturer's systematic influences the child is more likely than not to follow the directions set by the nurturer. However, this attitude is difficult to inculcate in thought, logic and reasoning and a love-oriented display of affection between the adult and the child (Cline, Foster and Jim Fay, 2006) is essential in order to imbue in the child to behave in the way as perceived by the caretaker.

However, as have mentioned before, there are several personal and situational determinants which influence the nurturing process. Mentioned here are a few prominent ones as observed by the nurtured child:

One fairly occurring personal influence is the hyperactive child. Hyperactivity in children is a generic occurrence in the behaviour displayed by the child, who most of the time reacts negatively to parental or the nurturant's instructions to the directions, modes and other controlling methodologies which come under the rubric of authoritarian behaviour emanating from the nurturant.

A child, who inherently develops behaviour that is sensitive to every change in the adult behaviour, is usually a hyperactive child. Not much can be done to change these attitudes and behaviour, but attempts can be made to modify this behaviour by anticipatory reactions by the adult and diverting the child's spontaneous channels to behave in a hyperactive manner (Linda, 1993).

Another commonly occurring situational determinant is that of a working mother. As the number of working mothers have increased over time in India, the conventional parenting practices are undergoing change and in many cases shared with other adults who are stay-at-home adults, caring for the household and other members of the family. Since, time is cut short, for the nurturant working mother to care for and to influence the child's development the development is a mixture of influences from other nurturing adults in the family. Therefore, the type of behaviour that emerges is usually a mix of two or more types, namely egalitarian, in a democratic or casual way. This type of inter-mix is likely to cause confused behaviour from time-to-time in the child's response.

Another type of interactive behaviour from the nurturer to the nurtured is one that indicates casualness. Part of the reason as to the appearance of casualness is a type of ideology which comes down from the nurturer's parental side while there are caring for her during her childhood with persistently unchanging modes of reaction that indicates casual behaviour. This happens to the extent that it is internalized by the child and becomes part of the child's personality output to treat everything in a casual manner. This casualness then becomes a totality of reaction not only with the caretaker, but also with other relatives in the family. For example, when the father returns from work he is most likely to ask the child that he had completed the day's homework. If the child says no, that I will not do it now, it is indicative of lack of commitment to the studies. If at any given time, the father is likely to punish the child because the child has not attended to the homework studiously, he is much reprimanded and, therefore, develops a dislike to homework. Perhaps, most children are not very enthusiastic to the completion of the day's homework when they return home after a hard day's of school. This dislike for the completion of the work set for the child then becomes an area of negativity for the child. Such children are not very keen to take up mathematics as a subject when they go to a higher school. Such a child is more likely to select easy subjects like Arts and Economics for work at the graduate level in a college.

Such children at the graduate level are likely to opt for sports as an option since this is also an outlet for the release of energy which otherwise the child will keep bottled up and become passively resentful.

For example, the conventional pattern of full-time maternal care of babies has been giving way in an increasing number of cases to day-care arrangements or employ domestic servants for the caretaking of the child while they are away at work during the day. Therefore, without much realization of the implications for the child that the child has, in fact, two caretakers, one during the day and one when the biological caretaker returns from work and who is more likely to be tired from work in the office and may not pay full attention enthusiastically to the child's completion of homework which enable mothers to continue in employment. This is a trend which has started in the Western World long time ago (Woodhead, 1987). In India, this change is especially true for mothers who have no choice, but to work in order to add an income to the family.

The working mother is by force unavailable for continuous parenting and often the child is left to his or her own devices and this non-nurtured process cultivate deviant tendencies which then is liable to become indelible characteristics as the child grows chronologically into becoming a young adult.

Another influence in causing variance in child behaviour is the differential personality behaviour between the mother and the father who might have differences about the way the child should be brought up. In many cases, the father tends to be authoritarian and restricted towards the child in following rules as compared to the female nurturer.

Another prevalent variable is differential ethnicity. For instance, if we move into a densely packed slum area in a metropolis, it will be seen as an assortment of people from different regional areas, speaking different languages, practising different social customs who then tend to form little ethnic groups within that slum area so that in a sense, there are little groups within the larger group of these slum dwellers.

Their daily lives are similarly in terms of living in the same geo-ecological area, but castes, ethnicity and religion vary even though there is a tendency for the 'like' to live next to the 'like' (to move towards other like-minded families where cultural practices are the same and there is little need for adjusting towards a different culture). A Bihari tends to search other Biharis to live close by so that there is equanimity in the type of culture practiced within the community. In such a way, a sense of identity is still preserved because of the equanimity among the families living in that particular community. Thus, eco-ethnicity is a very strong basis for similarities of cultural behaviour among the families in community living in a geo-ecological unit (Ravinder Kaur, 2001). Thus, bringing about members of families in the community to value and to look forward to the same kind of occupations as the rest of the adults in the neighbourhood. For example, in the slums where *jhuggi-jhoparis* exist, there is also a perception that the families are mostly similar in their ethos and values. Migrants in a slum area who live a dual pattern of livelihood, one in the urban slum and the other in their original habitat from where they migrated on a temporary basis to the urban are poters, where work exists to which they are accustomed, like poters *(Kumhars)*, who set-up a cluster of stalls doing the same kind of work and living similar kind of patterns of living. The parenting styles tend to merge one into the other because of the close proximity of living. The tendency is to try and not be too different from the neighbour, who come from a different State, except perhaps in their socio-religious customs. Because of the closeness of habitation of one with the other, parents are usually harassed in trying to survive and keep their jobs, since they are often transient in their ecological environment. The upbringing of child in these areas are haphazard where parents move from one style to another and it generally is amount authoritarian in the extreme since they do not have the time and leisure to monitor the child's behaviour. A great amount of casualness intervenes with these authoritarian practices.

If we move to a different spectrum of livelihood like those living in the upper socio-economic classes who are expected to be educated and know a little about social network of living, upbringing tends to be more of the democratic type, where there is time and opportunity to verbalize with the child, to monitor the child's behaviour and to take the time off to introduce the child to new ways of democratic living aided by the social media to which the family is exposed and, therefore, some part of the democratic style becomes embedded in the child's communication and behaviour. Since they are relatively well off, they are not pressurized by the lack of economic means in order to expose their children to the new ways of education, of living and for attempting to maintain or achieve higher standards of living. Therefore, they tend to use what are called the democratic ways of interaction in the family when they bring up their children, because they tend to take with them the style of upbringing that they have been exposed to in their childhood. Thus, there is a continuous circuit of the same type of living as many of their neighbours which are called *colonies*. However, since there tends to be parents who do not live in a situation where everything is in harmony, even amongst these upper class educated, there is a tendency of family disorganization, especially between the parents, who might have different perspectives on how to bring up a child. Apparently, the most strongest of all the variables affecting child upbringing as expected by the socio-economic class in which the family live is equanimity, equilibrium, similarity of values between the parents in relation to their interaction with the particular child. However, it must be stressed that all children in a particular family are nurtured in the same way as any of the other children as each child brings into the family his or her own ontogeny of behaviour which is part of their genealogical system.

In such upper socio-economic class families, too much is given too soon to the children so that these ups and downs affect the equilibrium between and among the parents and the child in adhering to any one standard of consistency. So, there might be several parents who are unhappy with their spouses or their in-law's interference and, therefore, their pattern of parenting might assume inconsistent forms such as a little bit of authoritarianism, a little bit of egalitarianism and perhaps a great deal of *laissez faire* or casualness in the upbringing of the child, which may be one style for one child in the family and different from other child in the same family. While the pattern of parenting emanating from the nurturer might be the same, the internalization by each of the children might be different simply because they bring to the situation their own inherent genealogical pattern of needs and aspirations as different from other children in the same family. Since they are involved in dealing with their own self-made pressures in meeting with their own problems, the different children have to act and react differentially among the children in their interactive processes.

It is possible that where both parents are working and the family lives a life of survival among the poor households in urban areas, and in rural areas, the parents are otherwise pre-occupied. The parent might be using a *laissez faire* style of interaction with the child or children, as they are not with them most of the time as they are more occupied in their occupational tasks.

There are also parentless children, namely, orphaned, abandoned and neglected, especially in the early years of childhood. Many street children probably come from homes where parenting is *laissez faire* and they have to eke out an existence in the company of their own gang, sleeping under flyovers or at railway or bus-stations and moving with the gang which forms a major surrogate parenting umbrella for the particular child.

Structures and Systems of Parenting Style in India

In analyzing parenting styles, one needs to ask the question as to what the parents expect of the child. Also, how does the parent act towards the behaviour exhibited by the child in relation to that she indicates as to the pathway along which she wishes the child to move towards her perceived goals for the child. How parents behave when they are disparaged when the behaviour of the nurtured does not meet with the goal envisualized by the nurturers? One can at once identify that the goal outcomes expected of the child is in a context, i.e. in a specific cultural context and, therefore, related to the societal norms of approved behaviour in the family and the community from which the family comes. Often it is the nurturer's family of orientation which consciously or unconsciously impels the nurturer to reinforce the kind of pathways or pathway the nurturer would wish for the nurtured. For instance, the goal towards which the adult attempts to direct child behaviour is related to societal norms of how the child ought to behave in specific situations, such as in the presence of visitors, in the classroom, in following the understood rules of the household such as times of bathing, eating and sleeping. Further, these expected types of behaviour are related to the direction in which the child's libidinal energy is repressed or re-directed. For instance, the child may want to hit his little brother because of a basic emotion of jealousy, and if the adult is aware of this the adult will try to redirect or repress this libidinal energy by offering a similar compensatory enactment of behaviour, which will redirect the child's behaviour, such as, giving the child a punching bag. It is known that it is not only the Freudian concept of redirection of energy but also the process of operant conditioning on the basis of the reinforcement theory, which indicates that if a certain type of behaviour is required such behaviour should be encouraged to appear and to be re-enforced or rewarded, either verbally or through offering materials they want. The child's behaviour is conditioned on being rewarded on an intermittent basis. For instance, if the adult's goal is that the child should learn to keep his school books neatly, then if the nurturant says can you put your books together and the child attempts to do so, the nurturant awards the child with words of approval such as, "that is well done". So, the next time when the child thinks of throwing his books around, he will remember how his mother/father had rewarded. The child is apt to repeat the previous behaviour which is constantly rewarded. Again the child observes the nurturant admiring the behaviour of a member of the family such as the husband and if the child belongs to the same sex, attempt to imitate the same behaviour of the male adult. According to the theoretical assumptions of the social learning theory, the child imitates the model admired and verbalized by the nurturant. However, ontogenetic rules indicate that the child has basic inherent needs different from that of the nurturant, and Maslow's theory indicates that if there is a gap between a need and its fulfilment, the child will strive to narrow the gap between the need and its required behaviour that can be observed. Finally, since the expected behaviour is within the parameters of the child's culture which is communicated to him through the channels of his family members (he tends to use the directed pathway), then the micro-ecosystem that is the family is an important source within the macro system of his society in terms of interpreting the cultural norms to the child (Bronfenbrenner, 1979). Erickson's theory on the life-cycle is an important focus as to the age at which the child develops and utilises positive social norms as expressed by the nurturer. This represents a certain positive behaviour which can be negated by his human environment such as the development of basic trust in infancy which, if repressed or misdirected, gives rise to basic mistrust of the child in his environment, both human and material (Erickson, 1977).

Child's Behavioural Compliance and Non-compliance in the Integration of the Child into the Family and Society

Perception is the inherent ability to use one's senses to clearly distinguish the features of an object perceived, whether it is through the senses of the visual, the auditory or any one of the other sensory abilities, either singly or in combination with each other. It is very important that both the adult nurturant and the nurtured child perceive the same object similarly and have the same need. For example, if the adult says to the nurtured child, would you give me the blue ball of wool, then both the colour and the configuration of the ball of wool must be visually seen as meant by the communicator, that is the adult, and internalized by the communicant (the child). There needs to be the same level of conceptualization between the adult who sends out a demand expression for the nurtured child to comply with and the conception of the nurtured child himself. Again, if the adult nurturant says the music you are playing is too loud, the pitch sensed by both the nurturant and the child should be the same in order that the child understand the nurturer's demand and direction (Maccoby and Martin, 1983).

Meaning and Importance of Parental Strategies

As is known parenting is a process which changes its direction from time-to-time as the adult perceives, pre-conceives and post-conceives about the expected behaviour of the child. Pre-conception is the inner feeling that the adult has about what should be done to bring about the effect of a possible goal in the child being nurtured, as perceived by the nurturer. As already stated before, the goal of the parent may not be the same as that perceived by the child. If there are differences on the perception of the goal by the nurturant and the child, then it is easier for the child to perceive the pathway and the goal indicated by the nurturer. There are very simple incidents in everyday life when these perceptions do not coincide like, for instance, the child wishing to see a movie (the child's perceived goal) with the parent wanting the child to complete a given task in the household like accomplishing his homework (the parents' perceived goal). When the perceptions do not coincide and, therefore, there is tangential perception between the two, then there is disharmony in the environment of the two actors. This, of course, happens in a one-to-one-relationship. It is to be remembered that these perceptions do not occur in a vacuum, but are perceived by both the nurturant and the child. If they are similar, then there is coincidence. If they are different, the child generally becomes resentful and resistant, and the nurturant has to think of a different pathway in order to coax or be forceful in saying that the child behaves as desired by the nurturant. Otherwise, the child would be ignored or pressurized in such a way that the child would be deprived of privileges. In the Western World, when the child does not comply, the nurturant would say, stand in that corner and do not move, or if wealthy, the child will be reprimanded by the nurturant, "go to your room and do not come out till I say so". Both the nurturant and the child are prompted by the motivations that arise from the ontogenetic pool of each of them and in relation to the environment in which both of them are able to, decode and to know what is to be done as perceived by each of them cognitively.

This occurs often with the interrupted interaction with others in the family. It may vary one from one adult to another. Very often the older child in whose care the young child becomes a mother surrogate and in the absence of the major caretaker, the mother, directs the child and is more punitive than the mother or the biological nurturer. In the Indian culture, it is to be remembered, that adult female relatives some times take the place of the mother and act as surrogates and in many cases, these substitute surrogates, might vary from one situation to another, as for instance, when the mother has to go on some important work, the child is left in the care of an aunt. With this variation in the type of techniques used by several caretakers on the same child from time-to-time, the child is expected to pivot his style of response such that the whole host of cues emanating from these various mother surrogates and, therefore, leads to confused response behaviour from the child. For instance, in a large family household, one child may wish to see a movie, another may wish to play football and the mother will certainly have different perceptions about the two siblings.

Therefore, variation in cues and responses does tend to indicate just one pathway and the child is expected to use the mode prescribed by each one of these mother surrogates and, therefore, shows behaviour that changes frequently from listening to authoritarian to discussing in a compromising way or ignoring the cues from the nurturant other than the mother. Eventually, the child internalizes the way he or she should behave differentially from one nurturant to another and several others who act as care taking surrogates.

The nature of such interactions increase exponentially when there are many siblings and one nurturant parent, or when there are many nurturing adults. Such contrasting perceptions increase the negativity in interaction and leads to vocalization of such feelings, where the child negates the parents' cues when the parent is authoritarian and the child is subject to negative responses emanating from the caretaker.

On the other hand, pre-conceived perception arises from the limited knowledge of the parent and the lack of knowledge of the child. Where such information reside in the caretaker's repertoire, the pre-conception of the parent imposes its restrictions on the child who does not know how to counteract these pre-conceptions and, therefore, is unprepared as to know what his reaction should be. Often, the nurturer and the child get entangled in tit-for-tat arguments where, because of the lack of preparedness, the parent overcomes the child's needs for doing other than what his nurturer directs him to do.

Further, post-conceived perceptions are those which are reflections on either side as to what is happening. During this post-perception period, feelings of either guilt or triumph occur when one of the individual succeeds in getting across the point of view expressed by him/her. A nurturers is able to comprehend what the child wishes to do and how to accommodate the need of the child without there being any antagonism, either in verbal communication or in bodily language of the adult nurturer or the child, and doing what he or she wants (parent or child) or when there is guilt for having done something that is not quite right. Sometimes, without much thought to the consequences, the nurturant might over-react in punishing the child negatively and as a consequence it frequently happens that the nurturer suffers from a sense of guilt for the over-reaction and, therefore, tries to make amends by appeasement in the situation.

The latter happens in most cases where the child is punished and the parents feel a sense of guilt for according to her ideology the nurturant having internalized the reactions of the child, begins to feel a sense of guilt that her instructions on her aspirations have had to be involved in any negative discussions with the child. The action and reaction between the two reaches a plateau of harmony. It has not resulted in a comfortable environment, especially guilt mixed with feelings of having done the right thing. These are, of course, inner feelings that are attached to the expression of these emotions. When there is resentment in the child the nurturant will try to placate the child and there is a post-placating situation invented by the nurturant. The child may say I do not want to, but eventually is forced to agree as other channels are withdrawn by the nurturant, still feeling resentment. On the other hand, the nurturer might find that she has been compelled to accede to the child's request without her really wanting to do so. And, therefore, retreats to creating a harmonious situation.

These illustrations on perceptions are further compounded by inter-personal perceptions, which usually remain in the unconscious, wherein the child tries to find a sense of conformity with the nurtuant's wishes mainly because there is a love-bonding between the nurturant and the child. Over a period of time, when such incidents are repeated and both the parent and the child know what is to occur before the incident occurs, the child may escape from it, the parent may persuade the child to comply with her aspirations as the nurturant has long term perspective as to what she perceives the child should become in terms of behaviour, aspiration and future acknowledgement of the directions that the nurturant gives to the child.

There are many other priorities during the period of nurturing process which the parent will use all over again so that it is finally internalized by the child. An example is that which is often heard when school children are talking during break time in school. One child who religiously follows parental directions will frequently say to her/his peers, "no, but my mother said, it should be done this way," repeating the continuous reinforcement made by the nurturant. These expressions and counter-expressions are part of the conscious and unconscious mechanisms of the mind of both the parent and the child except that the parent has much more experience and, therefore, much more power over the interpersonal perceived directions. However, it is not always that the parent has an explanation in terms of his interpersonal perception. A young child may ask the difficult question like how are babies born (which is difficult to explain by the nurturant because it is too difficult to be understood by the child). The parent has the knowledge but not the perceptual ability to know how to explain it to the child and the child through experience (during the chronological period of growth into an adolescent) will eventually learn (what it means) to put across questions to his parents that he has perceived they would be unable to explain to him in the terms of his level of understanding. In order to avoid a lengthy explanation, the composition of which the child is not able to comprehend, the nurturer does away with the lengthy explanation by saying that because I say so, or that is how it is. The usual explanation from the parent is because I say so or that is how it is or it does not need to be understood for you to do it. From these types of expressions, one can make out the rigidity (or elasticity) of parental perceptions where they do not have the perceptual space to monitor and manipulate a situation so that their point of view overcomes the expected interpersonal perception of the child.

These are internally inherent abilities of the parent and the child where parental power has more control over directing perceptions whether pre-conceived, ongoing, post-conceived or inter-personally conceived. Internal perceptions are usually congruent with the child's level of cognition and it is important that the nurturant communicates an explanation congruent with the child's level of cognitive understanding. Therefore, the fulcrum of the differentiation between the parental expression and interaction with the child is much more wide-ranging (in terms of capacity than that which accrues to the child's level of understanding) than that of the child whose experience depends upon his chronological maturity. Therefore, the two important *modus operandi* are depth of experience and chronological maturity (and the way the nurturer uses language which is simplisitic and so can be easily comprehended by the child) and the ways in which parents use strategies to interact with their children. However, until and unless these are well-known (and easily utilized by the nurturant these strategies or practices may not have the desired impact as anticipated by the nurturant), well-entrenched and automatic reactions to the child, they may also not be successful for strategies depend upon the next fulcrum and that is the goal of the parent *vis-à-vis* the goal of the child. The combination, therefore, of chronological maturity of the child, experiential ability of the parent to know what and how the explanation should meet the cognitive ability of the child are two important factors in creating a harmonious interaction between the two. These pivotal factors arrange and re-arrange the strategies that parents use in dealing with their children. It stands to reason, therefore, that the more knowledgeable and, therefore, the more educated the parent, whether educated institutionally or educated through accumulation of experiences, the more easily the nurturant knows at what level she should direct her communication so that it is cognitively and verbally communicated so that the child is able to comprehend and react positively. The strategies are used depending more upon the goal direction of the parent rather than the child because the nurturant has better ability to foresee in prognostic manner as to what the child's behaviour would be like. In other words, the parent is the director and the child is the directed individual. Naturally, the older the child the more he or she is able to debate, discuss, disagree with the parent, relating to the aspirations of the nurturant to his own perceived goals. However, a child may be well-developed in age, progression but may be living in an environment which does not expand his horizon of knowledge, as for instance, a child living in a village or hamlet in a tribal area *vis-à-vis* the child in a highly sophisticated metropolis and, therefore, may be unable to manipulate or monitor the strategies that his parent uses and, therefore, fails in his attempts to reach his goals successfully. A village child does not know anything more than that he sees, that is, which is happening in and around him and he, therefore, learns what is available from the tribal or rural occupations in his environment to use as his future skills in his later life. For example, the child may learn to become a good carpenter because he comes from a community of which the traditional occupation is carpentry. Similarly is the case with the children of potter communities. For example, in Delhi there is a locality near a place called Saket, which has a whole host of potters displaying their wares and the host of potters is becoming a community in itself. However, if the child has a high cue-grasp and his intelligence level is much more than that of his parents; his curiosity will compel him to look beyond their own community parameters and to search for professions that are better paying and more complicated. To take another example, in the city of Hissar in Haryana, there were families who went around selling metal-made buckets and such like items, going around on cycles. Eventually, over a couple of generations one such family has become a multimillionaire family.

This might lead to educate the nurtured and the nurturer or a compromise. The child from such a low socio-economic class may be a high-skilled genius in a technology in a potential manner. But parameters of his environment may not give him an opening to look out and explore the outer world and, therefore, his skills remain dormant (unless he himself feels the need to achieve and, therefore, pushes himself to attain a higher standard). But given the opportunity, there is always the possibility of moving from "rags to riches" if the child's initiative and his achievement-motivation are high enough to break the barrier of belonging to a lower socio-economic class. Therefore, an important hypothesis here is the child's high motivation level and a high self-esteem, living in a highly motivated family. The child can then achieve to be much more developed than the original status from which the child came. This is coupled with another hypothesis, namely, the ability and the aspiration of the nurturer to motivate the child to achieve by being democratic in interaction and in explaining to the child the various *modus operandi* by which the child can raise his cognitive power to comprehend his need to achieve and the reinforcement given to him by the adults around him.

This is not to say that parents are almost always more learned or need-oriented to reinforce the child to improve his status. In an authoritarian environment, one might hypothesize that the attempt is to retain the child in the same traditional occupation as of the parents, or of the family or community in which they live. This can often become setting up of limitations to the achievement of the nurtured child. Sometimes, unknowingly, the parents open the window of such expressions of the child, but in most cases to protect their own security they tend to limit the child to what they know in their own environment. Therefore, a further variable and perhaps overriding the interactive strategies of perception, of goal-direction, of accumulation of experiences, is the dominating characteristics of the personality of the nurturer and the pressures of the family around the nurturer. Therefore, when there is the need to analyze the nurturant and nurtured, it is also necessary to analyse the various interactive variables that afflict the cognitive development of the child and the parenting style of the nurture. These two combine to state an important hypothesis that the congruence or incongruence between the nurturer and the nurtured is what propels the child to develop a perception of pro-operative opportunities to development, to be furthered or to be inhibited by the retributions of the nurturant.

From an analysis of what is written above, one can deduce five important concepts impinging upon the interaction between the nurturer and the child:

(a) The relative predictability of the personality of the child and the nurturer are the crucial aspects.
(b) Given particular situational determinants, the unpredictable or predictable nurturant's interaction with the child and the child's nature to respond to the parental cues in different situation, points out to the repeated or changing nature of the sources from which the personality and the situational determinants impinge upon the development of the child.
(c) The limitations of the chronological age of the child, and the wisdom of the parent which can make for the compatibility or incompatibility in the interaction between the two individuals, namely the nurturer and the nurtured.
(d) The next most important are the desired goals of the child and the aspirations or lack of aspirations on the part of the nurturer.
(e) The environment of other adults in and around the child and the nurturer which interacts in influencing the child's development, either positively or negatively, or inconsistently both, in varying degrees.

Given the above, however, it is quite evident that it is the power of the dominance of the parent that pervades the nurturance situation (i.e. the whole environment of the parent-child interaction and the fine-nuances which are obtained from them). The personality of the parent is dependent upon several factors, but more especially upon his or her own childhood experiences, which she brings to bear on her own nurturing processes in the management of the upbringing of her child. If the parent has lived under a regime of strictness where her own nurturer has been very authoritarian, of limitation in activities of lack of communication with adults or others in the family, the tendency is to carry over these characteristics in the caretaking of her own child, as these are foundational characteristics which have meaning for the parent in perceiving her own characteristics and those of the nurtured herself as the nurturer. There are times when the child is more frequently negative at times, or more positive at other times, the child is moulded into showing behaviour as such. However, when there is variation between the positivity and negativity, the child develops a confused identity. Having been exposed more frequently to either end of the dimension, because the nurturant has been very strictly or negatively brought up, the nurturer as a parent would tend to act differently, namely much more leniently when she was a child.

Personality theories as indicated in the book *'Development of Personality in the Indian Ecology'*, influence the caretaker's self-perceived needs for the child. There is a tendency to be 'either or' in the description of the child's behavioural development.

However, theories remain theories only in so far as they are guidelines. In so far as social realities they are permutated and convoluted to become a mixture of several theories. For example, Erikson says that later adolescence is a period where the child strives to attain his identity or becomes confused about it. He or she carries this underlying characteristic along with himself or herself when they themselves become parents and implement the process of upbringing that they are acquainted with, i.e. the kind of personality development the child grows into is more influenced by the caretaking adult than by anybody else, in the making of his personality. As a consequence of growing up chronologically into adolescents and becoming young adults, the nurturant child develops his or her framework of behaviour. They are some times able to identify themselves as "yes, I am doing the right thing as a parent, because I know how my own personality has been developed under the influence of my own caretaker, namely the nurturance given to the mother during her childhood." I know that I should be a good mother, giving the right nurturance in terms of morality, knowledge and behaviour related to them which I have learned during my own childhood. It is to be a good law-abiding citizen, believe and teach my religious norms to my children, control their expressions and behaviour and such like. At other times, it is possible that the caretaker might be in doubt as to whether following the impact of her own mother is good for the child or not. This type of vacillating behaviour in the nurtured child might be due to the mother's own vacillation as a child, which she inadvertently transfers to her own child in the nurturing process. For example, when the child becomes an adolescent, the caretaking nurturer might be confused whether the adolescent child should move around freely with his peer group or whether he should be restricted; whether he ought to insist that his primary school child does his homework whole day or let him go off at times to the mall. In this, the caretaker might be affected by the mores of the society around her. She might be very scared as to what the society will say if his child does the "wrong thing".

A prominent extraneous factor which could influence the caretaker's interaction with a particular nurtured child could be the effect of the sibling rivalry, which jostles for the attention of the caretaker to themselves, thus impeding the one-to-one relationship between the nurturer and the particular nurturant in the family.

As the child grows older, the overpowering influence of the peer group might be much more forceful than the one-to-one interaction between the nurturer and the nurturant.

It is necessary to identify single parent households and multiple nurturance in a given household. In these two situations, multiple reactions might take place without the nurturing parent being aware that these different types of nurturance could affect the one-to-one relationship between an identified nurturer and the nurturant. In single family households, mother may find it a burden in trying to raise the child on her own, whereas there is multiple mothering as in an orphanage or in a household where there are multiple mothers, there could very well be confused interaction between the nurturant and the child for the simple reason that by the many surrogate mothers the child might be influenced differentially by each one of the different nurturers.

The major generic attribute transferred to the nurtured child is the cultural pattern which surrounds the family, the household and the community impinging upon the nurturant to subscribe to the same social religious moral beliefs passed down from generations which the nurturing parent carries with her.

The Characteristics of the Nurturant

The major nurturant may be one or more than one. For instance, the biological mother is the most major of all nurturants since she has given birth to the child; in other situations the nurturants may be a combination of the mother and the father where both take care of the child, especially when they are working parents. There are others who are combinations of one, two or more. For example, the mother surrogate may be an aunt or a grandmother, a combination of mother, aunt and grandmother, an older sibling or even a far-removed relative where some times motherless children are sent to be looked after. In several instances, the child may be just an institutionalized child, put into a children's home since there is no one to take care of the child. The child is exposed not only to a variety of nurturance, but different nurturants at different times. Thus, it is obvious that there are a host of nurturants, some times singly or jointly. It stands to reason that when there is more than one nurturants, the pattern used by the nurturers are a combination, where some times the child is exposed to one and not another, and may be for different periods of time. There is also the phenomenon when the child is, relatively speaking, born of one parent and then when her parents are divorced, separated or have demised, goes to the home of one or the other. In these circumstances of divorce and re-marriage, the child is exposed to different styles of nurturance, namely, by the biological mother at one time and the step-mother at another time or more than one female. In the upper echelons of society, there is much divorce and remarriage and, at times, remarriage is more than once. The child is, therefore, shuttled from one situation to another and, if under court custody, is required to spend at some times with the remarried mother and some times with the remarried father. These changes naturally cause contradictions in the influences in the nurturing processes between the old and the new mother and a variety of mothers. The child is influenced by this variety at different times; different messages are sent to the child when he or she is moved from one home to another, creating confusion as to his/her identity.

When there is a joint family, the child is exposed to different nurturers at different times. In these situations, there may be differing nurturing processes for the same child who then gets exposed by these differences and is unaware of the differing nature of such influences. Interpretations given through commands and demands from one of the multiple mothers to another, causes the child to retreat from obeying the other since the child has had a different directional call from the second. There will be several occasions when this will occur especially in the joint household system found mainly in rural areas or in congested urban slums, where space is insufficient and there is need to live as close together as possible.

Thus, we see that to a parent, the child calls for different forms of nurturance dependent upon his knowledge as to how the nurturant reacts, and depending upon his remembrance of his reaction he tends to deploy. This repeated cue and response communication between the nurturant and the child is the growing repertoire of similar communications with the nurturant. It forms repetitive type of communications with which the child becomes familiar.

The child's personality is also differentially affected and gives rise to many different kinds and strands of personality expression. It is essential to remember that beneath all this nurturing processes are several phylogenetic and ontogenetic traits of two or more than two different individuals, namely, the adult nurturants and the nurtured child. These bring about several different styles of interaction, for it is not just that the mother is a major influencing factor, but some times the child can also use the situation to insert as response those repeated responses with which he is familiar with the nurturant. For example, from childhood when the nurturnats asks the question of the child the child tends say: "*Ahen*" (to mean "yes") and when he wants to say something negative, he will immediately use the words "no, no", or as a protest will begin to cry. This is especially so during early childhood and primary school years. Remembering that these ontogenetic traits are as different as apples and oranges, the prediction of who will overwhelm the other is uncertain, because it may just be that the stronger character prevails over the weaker. For example, a mother may insist that the child go to bed early and the child may be defiant, the tantrums ensue and the mother may give in from sheer exhaustion of having to insist while she knows that all the time she may have a lurking situation that she is not going to succeed. She has a nurturing awareness. Thus, in a way, the child may be the winner and the mother the loser. On the other hand, the mother may not give in (and waits till the child finally gives in, ending with "if you say sorry, I will let you have the toy, but you must not break it"). She may physically punish the child so that through sheer helplessness the child sobs himself to sleep. Therefore, when parenting styles are described, it is like adjusting the cloth to fit the person. In other words, to style a pattern of adjustment by the nurturer or by the child, or by both, is attuned or patterned according to the situation and according to the dominant or recessive personalities. For this reason, the nurturance methods are called styles in order to indicate that they are different styles and more often than not one style is more dominant with the adult and for that reason, it is called autocratic or authoritarian or even most predominant. These are synonyms. In the same way, when the adult is using placating or persuading terms, and is willing to listen to the child's needs and, therefore, gives in to his needs, this style is called democratic or interactively permissive. Yet another style is one where the nurturing adult is careless about how she would respond and, therefore, ignores the child's response and this response is called *laissez faire* or the unresponsive non-dominant and non-caring, hoping that at some time the child would respond positively, instead of ignoring the cue given by the nurturant parent. Each of the countless parenting styles dynamically differ from the other, but the particular style used by the nurturant constantly reflects the dominant characteristic of the dominant individual, which in most cases is the adult nurturer. Parenting styles cannot be cohesed with parenting practices, because practices relate to the common child-rearing methods such as weaning, toilet-training and such like every-day episodes which becomes common features in the way the child is reared. Therefore, styles relate more to the communication and other interaction that is a common feature of the nurturer's interaction with the nurturant and *vice versa*, which then dominates all features of child-rearing techniques imposed by the nurturer on the child—autocratic or persuasive (democratic) or non-imposing (*laissez faire*). A parenting practice is the way a specific situation is attended to by the parenting nurturer at any given time, whereas, a parenting style is the continuous and repeated way in which the child is tackled or nurtured by the nurturant. It seems plausible, therefore, to assume that a parenting style is a combination of differential practices used in various combinations which are typical of the nurturant (Nancy and Laurence, 1993), which reflect the particular style.

As early as in 1966, Baumrind (1966) described two completely different styles of child rearing and although there were no empirical data they served to picturize two major different types—the permissive parent and the authoritative parent—and their differential effects on the child being nurtured. In a sense this can be equated with what is known as the two different types of behaviour, for the reason that the third imposing style is democratic and applies more to the situations which evolve between the nurturant and the nurturer where the nurturer makes the effort to discuss with the child while a particular reaction like agreeing with the parent or arriving at a solution is something agreeable to both the nurturant and the nurturer. There have been many different explanations, descriptions and new hypotheses about the interactive patterns of behaviour between the nurturer and the nurturant and the presumed effect of parental patterns of child behaviour. For example, the egalitarian, the *laissez faire* and the authoritarian styles have been enunciated by Lewin, Lippitt and White (1939) in their experiment with school children. However, what has been observed is that it is not an easy process to attach parental behaviour attitudes and communicated values with the child's behaviour. The description needs observance of the repetitive style of the parent and the repetitive response of the child, to arrive at an identity as to what the parental style is. The variation that occurs eludes description because there is no one type of adult behaviour that influences the child behaviour because each has a circumstantial context which is not often repetitive. However, taken the recurrence of the nurturant's repetitive style, it may be assumed that this style is the most predominant interactional process with the child. For example, in a context where a child has to complete his homework, one situation might be that the child is watching television. Another situation might be that the child is playing again and does not want to leave it. Another might be that the child is not inclined to study and so on. Each such situation is in a differential context. On the other hand, the adult might be in a differential mode every time that the child is required to do his homework. Therefore, it is not only the individual that is in a different mode every time, but that the situational determinants might change from time-to-time. For these reasons, it is not possible to study any one parental style of interaction with the child as being a typically repetitive behaviour.

Therefore, it is important that one should study the bases of the psychological interpretation whether of the nurturant or the nurtured as to how they co-jointly interact and under what circumstances. They make up a situation where the parenting style of the nurturant can be detailed. There are, however, a few basic principles which underlie this interactive behaviour between the adult and the child. These are:

- Instrumental competence. means the ability of the nurturant and the nurturer to come to terms with the given situation.

- Internalization of the anticipated behaviour of the child depends upon the ability of the nurturer to be able to decipher in a proactive manner what response of the child would be and act accordingly.
- The appropriate communication and its understanding from the adult to the child and *vice versa*.
- The type of instrumental behaviour which is the goal of the parent, expected by the nurturer from the nurturant, namely the child—whether it is uni-dimensional, bi-dimensional or multi-dimensional in the solution to the given situation of interaction.
- The emotional understanding between the adult and the child, whether negative or positive, which can cause a coming together of the nurturer and the child or a negative atmosphere of their interaction.

From the above it is clear that any one of the above may interact with one or both in different combinations at any one time. For example, the adult might expect a certain competence from the child which the child can or cannot comply with. Added to this, there may be communication of differential goals, which is the basis of the disharmony between the adult nurturant and the child. Above and beyond all these, however, are the differential ontogenetic inherent abilities. The goal of the parent might be, for instance, that the child achieves a certain level academically, which is not achievable since perhaps the IQ of the child is not able to function in such a manner as would indicate the achievement aspired to by the nurturer, or the child does not have the potential to rise to the expected level of goal performance as expected by the nurturer.

Since the basis of interaction of the nurturant with the nurtured is sourced from the bedrock of emotionality, it is essential to understand the meaning of emotionality. Emotionality is an inward excitation in relation to another human being/object. In the context of parenting styles, it refers to what we call "*mamata*" or motherliness, consideration, gentleness and wanting to take care of another human being in a nurturant manner. Emotionality, of course, in this sense is positive, like love, compassion, harmony, togetherness, and the like. It can also be negative, like anger, jealousy, wrath, and loss of temper. Female adults in the caring of their progeny usually display a great deal of "*mamata*', but when provoked can also display negative emotions such as not rewarding behaviour, anger and punishing the nurtured.

According to ancient Hindu scripture "*Rasadhyaya*", there are nine basic emotions.

The primary emotions are:

- Sorrow (*shoka*),
- Anger (*krodha*),
- Sexual passion, love or delight (*rati*), and
- Amusement, laughter, humour or mirth (*hasya*).

These above four are primary emotions in that they are an expression of attitude or feeling.

Secondary emotions are:

- Fear or terror (*bhaya*),
- Disgust or disillusion (*jugupsa*),
- Amusement or recreation (*manoranjan*),
- Astonishment, Wonder, or Amazement (*vismaya*), and
- Serenity or calmness (*sama*).

Much of Sanskrit philosophy elevated the human mind and body to the status of sacramental objects. The famous sixth chapter of the *Natyashastra* is about the narrative structure (the causes, consequences and concomitants) of the above basic emotional states and the most effective means of their representation is the facial expression, voice, posture, setting, characterization and physiological response (Richard, Shweder *et al.*, 2008).

These expressions in Hindu lifestyle are related to the goals of life. One of these goals is pleasure (*kama*) related to physical passion; the second goal, which is control of power, is related to anger; the third goal—social duty and moral virtue (*dharma*)—is linked to perseverance; the fourth goal—salvation (*moksha*)—is the highest goal and is linked to serenity.

Emotions depend upon the social and moral context in which these behaviours are expressed. The feelings and expressions of emotions are related, in psychology, to the Freudian pleasure-pain principle. Pain is exhibited by the moving away from the source of pain, while pleasure is associated with the attraction towards the object of pleasure, real or symbolic.

Emotions on the basis of characteristics of an individual can be nurtured from the early stages onwards and modulated in socially acceptable expressions, which then becomes societal norms as the chronological age of the child increases. A newborn's cry denotes pain and smile denotes pleasure. These inherent expressions of emotion are modulated according to the moral characteristics of the society where certain behaviours are considered good and, therefore, expected to be pleasurably accomplished; while others are societally negated and, therefore, to be attritioned or suppressed.

The importance of emotionality in the package of nurturance is, therefore, extremely significant because not only is it a natural characteristic of the nurturant, but that it is also related to socio-religious norms of behaviour which are the bases of fundamental socialization processes imbibed in the nurturant. Emotionality is not regularly homogeneous or is continuous, but is intermittent from negative to positive and *vice versa* (dependent upon the cues from the adult nurturer), according to chronological age and is much more expressed in the female sex than in the male and can be promoted or restrained depending upon the individual's personality (Brody, Leslie, 1999).

Emotionality is fundamental in human expression; and is closely interwoven in human attitudes. This basic characteristic is also significant in terms of socio-religious normative behaviour which is explainable in the way the nurturant guides the behaviour of the nurtured towards societal norms.

Cognition is based on an understanding of perception. Perception is the knowledge of what is observed by the senses and is a process of maturity development which occurs through the chronological stages from early childhood. It grows from simple to complex form as experiences are accumulated. Accuracy of perception is basic to the process of cognition. Attached to emotionality, it is essential that the cognition of the idea of object is understood in the same manner by both the nurturant and the nurtured, so that the interactional processes are harmonious.

Cognition is, therefore, intertwined with the accuracy of perception when the nurturant says to the nurtured: "this behaviour will not be tolerated by me". It is essential that the nurtured understand that the object, namely the nurturant is negatively attuned to cues emanating from the nurturer.

The important aspects of cognition arise from the development of the following:

(1) Epigenesis which implies maturation of the individual over time and space in developmental experience, mainly through the process of cognitive maturation (Gottlieb, 2003).
(2) Given the phylogenetic basis, demarcation of individualists' morphology within the species occurs, and in this instance, it is the human being.
(3) This differentiation takes place on the basis of the splitting of the homogenetic fundamental characteristics of the species into heterogeneous entities, bearing the same general characteristics, but including other unique characteristics specific to the inherent nature, capacities of the species.
(4) Heinz Werner indicates that development proceeds from a state of globality and lack of differentiation to a state of increasing differentiation, articulation and the hierarchical integration (Werner, 1957) of the cognized experiences.
(5) There is a relationship between cause and effect indicating the importance of causality in evoking a cognized experience.
(6) The increasing complexity of sensory stimulation stimulates the interactivity of neurons to attain higher levels of interaction, therefore, leading to higher levels

of cognition which is exhibited in the spoken communication from the nurturant to the nurtured.

(7) Probabilistic epigenetic development is based on a probability that one set of interactive behaviour has the probability to lead on to a higher set of more probable complex understanding of the spoken word from the nurturant or from the nurturant's behaviour which the child by imitation adds to his combination of previous experiences to more complex understanding of the spoken words.

(8) Genetic neural behaviour and environmental interactivity form the foundational parameters of development, both physical and mental.

(9) Differential and multiple consequences can arise from causative cues which can be reflected or not reflected by the nurtured child.

The above indicate the paradigm of the biological and neurological bases of cognition. Developmental psychologists and more pronouncedly Piaget have worked on the neuro-psychological bases of cognition which proceeds to unfold over the chronological stages, from the stage of sensory motor development to the stage of formal operations (Piaget, 1929). In the expanding sphere of cognitive development, the nurtured is guided through experiential learning of the pathways indicated by the nurturer. The nurturer's special unique style influences the unfolding of the inherent characteristics of the child. This is done by directing and monitoring the pathways that the nurtured should take as guided by the nurturant. For example, a mother whose characteristics are predominantly one of ordering, demanding and insisting (authoritative) tends to demarcate in a rigid fashion the parameters within which the nurtured child should behave. This behaviour is consciously or unconsciously in the direction of the goals envisualised by the nurturer, who then monitors the behaviour of the child to follow the directed mode of behaviour she tries to instil in the nurtured child. At times, the mother may be lackadaisical and allow the child to do what he perceives and cognizes as a type of behaviour that meets his needs and moves towards his own perceived goals in as much as they suit his inherent needs. It is difficult to correlate parental techniques with the outcomes or goals envisualised by the nurturer in relation to child behaviour because both vary on the basis of many unknown variables specific to each personality and in each situation. Therefore, it requires careful observation to correlate parental expectations with the outcome of the expected behaviour of the child as there is variability both parent-wise and child-wise in terms of their personality, which acts and reacts as determined by the cues from the nurturer to the child and *vice versa*. Therefore, at this juncture it is necessary to query, "what are the underlying theoretical bases of the interactive mode of communication between the nurturer and the child?" This is essential to make some acceptable hypotheses as mere descriptions of behaviour can be just conjectures. Idiographic case studies are usually a one-time description of behaviour and may not be generalized to typical behaviour patterns in a homogenous group of individuals as there is more variation among the individuals rather than a conglomerate description of a group. In other words, nomothetic data are essential to find homogeneity within varying individual parenting by the nurturer. This is especially essential if we are to differentiate one parenting style from another. In other words, it is essential to have some acceptable theoretical hypotheses from which we can offer certain reliable descriptions of behaviour outcomes in the nurtured's behaviour as dependent upon the nurturer's cues, verbal or non-verbal. The more repeated the cues the more likely that the nurtured child would tend to follows these cues emanating from the nurturer.

The discussion on parenting styles in this book leads one to analyze the changes that have occurred in the parenting styles during the course of the years passed by. In the present Chapter, the changes in parenting styles are discussed with reference to the two concepts, viz. modernization and globalization. Modernization has generally been defined by social scientists as an all-encompassing process of cultural and socio-economic changes, whereby the developing societies seek to acquire some of the characteristics common to industrial Societies (Haviland, 2002). According to Bright (2000), through modernization, traditional societies attempt to adapt themselves culturally, economically and politically to the requirements of the contemporary world. In the course, traditional knowledge and techniques give way to the application of scientific knowledge derived mainly from the West. Due to modern technology, modernization creates changes in traditions and values. People adopt new traits and trends as the traditional agrarian societies transform into industrial societies. Due to industrialization and its concomitant process of urbanization, families tend to move towards centrifugal tendencies as the traditional economic homogeneity among family members dissolves when the individual members of families tend to seek non-agricultural jobs. Education plays a significant role in this diversification of occupations. As family members increasingly gets engaged in separate and independent occupations, they tend to break away from family restrictions in the quest for individual freedoms. Cumulative effect of this process has been the gradual break-down of the traditional joint family system and the setting up of nuclear families. In this transformation, the choices available for upbringing and nurturing of the young generation have distinctly changed. In the traditional joint family system, there were more adult members available for monitoring the nurturing and socialization process and because of the conservative societal values, the young ones of families were supervised and controlled by the adult members in the joint or extended families. Thus, it can be seen that the parenting styles in the traditional family system in India has been mostly authoritarian. This was in part because of the situational determinants of the traditional joint family system. These situational determinants of joint families were availability of more adult members to supervise the upbringing of children in accordance with the family and societal values. As the joint families were based on agrarian economies, the corresponding family values were conservative. With the coming of nuclear families, the situational determinants have changed. The number of members available for parenting the young ones has become limited to immediate biological parents, or at the most the elderly grandparents. Apart from this structural change in the family, there have also been changes in values and aspirations for the children. As the strictness in the control loosened, the parenting style has tended to become more of "authoritative" in nature. What this means is that the parents are increasingly realizing the need to be responsive to the demands of the children. This implies the introduction of a democratic element in the parenting practice. This democratization can be seen to be corresponding with the socio-political values of modern society, among the defining features of which are the norms and values which emphasise openness, democracy, participation and entrepreneurship (Parsons, 1967; Smelter, 1969).

Globalisation, which can be viewed as the latest phase of the modernization process, has further deepened and widened the restructuring of families and family relationships. The Indian rural society has especially been affected by the rapid changes brought about by the globalization and its important aspects of information technology and demographic changes. Demographic changes have occurred not only due to migration of rural people to urban areas but also significant movement of people from one country to another for trade and work. Such increases in the movement of goods, labour, and services have brought about changes in the relationship in the communities. This change is reflected in the concept of the "global village", the emergence of which has been contributed by various social and cultural interactions among the people beyond the traditional boundaries of communities and even nation States. Among the negative aspects of the globalization processes are family disruption and the increasing social and domestic violence. Competitiveness associated with globalization has exacerbated individualism and a movement away from emotional bonding with one's own communities. The changes have affected people's identities and cultural values. Some of the new values, especially individualism, have tended to cause dissonance and conflict with existing deep-rooted values.

This tendency has the potential for creating a global society which is not ordered because of the lack of regulating norm. Durkheim postulated this state of disorder by the concept of "anomie", resulting from the potential scourge of modern competitive society. The manifestations of this disorderly state are unrestricted desires, insatiable appetites, unconstrained behaviour, and general feelings of irritation and dissatisfaction. A strong and ordered society can only be guaranteed where beliefs and behaviours are properly regulated by socialization, which is a process whereby individuals learn to conform to society's prevailing norms and values. In the past, the young generations were socialized to conform to the society. It used to be said that the people were socialized through society. In this background, it is a pertinent question to ask, "what are the societal values that the parents need to inculcate in the younger generation given that the society itself is undergoing rapid changes?"

The authoritative parenting combines both the authoritarian control and the liberalizing tendency of allowing democratic participation in decision-taking. If we relate this model with modernization, we can see some times modernization having negative change in society. People are socialized through their society and the society changes individual behaviour with the passage of time.

Joint family property tends to be disrupted since its individual adult members are being increasingly engaged in different occupations. Because of this reason they are unable to reside together. The family members break away from the family restrictions. They develop their own initiatives for independence. The inevitable result is the weakening of the family authority, family ties and the family itself.

It can be observed that these aspects of modernization have changed the situational determinants and consequently the personal determinants of parenting styles.

Parenting styles and practices are culturally shaped and hence vary across societies. In the present context of economic and cultural globalization and its corollary demands on families, parents in the contemporary Indian society are being compelled to reorient their socialization precepts and practices to reconcile the traditional and modern cultural values, especially during adolescence. There is a dissonance in living a balanced life when culturally rooted traditional values are juxtaposed with the modern values arising from a globalised world. In this context, there are compelling reasons for parents to adopt parenting mechanisms which make up a compromise between the traditional and modern.

In the ultimate analysis, globalization can be said to be a process of culmination of modernization. Globalisation has different aspects. Among them, those which have closest bearing on changes in parenting styles are economic, demographic, occupational, and cultural.

The parents will continue to use the positive aspects of the traditional patterns of upbringing even after the modernizing changes. The parents of the next generation will try to use parts of their own childhood upbringing experiences while they are bringing up their own children. Sometimes, the kind of upbringing aspects which they cherish from their childhood, they tend to use repeatedly and some unpleasant characteristics they tend to drop aside. Which ones will predominate is anybody's guess. However, the fact remains that the individual adult will vacillate from one to the other according to the perception of the individual in the cognition that a part of a past life figures well in the future upbringing of the child. For this reason, these personality and situational determinants will occur from time-to-time, depending upon the impact that they have on the adult caretaker's mental attitudes, values and more especially goal-directed behaviour, which are generally part of the adult individual's repertoire.

Cultural globalization has had its effects on parenting styles (Sanagavarapu, 2010). Parenting practices of families who live or lived in other countries are hybridized as they try to adapt to the cultural differences between the country of the origin and the new country. This has important consequences for children's development and early childhood practices.

Thus, traditional patterns of parenting are undergoing change under the influence of various factors engendered by modernization and globalization. One of the important features is the change in the ecology in which the parents nurture and socialize their children. What these changes mean is that the situational determinants are different from those existed in the past. Technological developments have played an important role in bringing about this change.

These have resulted in changes in parental values and goals the parents set for their children which are critical determinants of parenting behaviour (Dornbusch *et al.*, 1987).

Cultures and their characteristics are usually quite stable for a long period of time. This means that, within cultures, socio-cultural systems have been established that have proved successful for long-term adaptation to their ecological conditions and settings. This stability can be achieved only through successful socialisation of the younger generation by the older generation; by which the necessary behaviour conforming to the social norms, skills, competence, and values are developed and transmitted to the next generation (Holden & Buck, 2002).

In the traditional Indian families, parents seek to develop a number of attributes in their children: (1) positive self-concept, (2) perceptive self-correction, (3) self-control, (4) self-confidence, (6) humble and pious disposition, (7) competency in conflict resolution, and (8) family solidarity.

What do the parenting styles indicate if one were to unravel them and place them in the appropriate relationship considering their varying aspects? They would consist of the psychological aspects of the person's characteristics of being amenable or otherwise to the individual's interacting with each other, or being confident or otherwise and such like. Together with social aspects of being aware of social norms and behaviour and acting as related to them or otherwise, the individual is also aware of the environment in which he or she operates, namely, the general economic and social environment and the specific environment in which the individual is interacting with, such as the market place, a garden, a carnival, and, for children, the playground. The individual may also be aware of the shortcomings, both of himself and of his environment. For example, his inability to act as a modern parent which he wishes to be, but has limitations to do so. There will be many situations where the child will not be with the nurturant and will be mostly at school or in a hostel.

Parenting implies a constant ongoing process when the parent and the child are in interaction physically or mentally. Often there are breakages in this interaction, for example, when the child becomes a hostel student. When the child comes back to his parents, then the parents needs to reconnect with the child. By this time, the child has obviously accumulated a number of experiences.

The ideal style of parenting is that of constant and consistent interaction between the parents and the child. It is one that is non-threatening and persuasive. Taking a holistic concept, the parent is crisscrossed by other experiences during the parenting period.

Earlier psychologists like Baumrind and Nancy Darling have structured their conception of the parenting style around the implications of what is meant by authoritative and authoritarian styles and have tended to emphasize that parenting styles are first and foremost indicated by the ideology of the parent. These psychologists have defined parenting style as "a complex activity that includes many specific behaviours that work both individually and together to influence child outcomes" (Nancy Darling, 1999). Later, human development psychologists have emphasized parenting processes more clearly as being one of socialisation with emphasis simultaneously on the characteristics of the socialisers and socialisees with special emphasis on the behaviour of the socialisee as being mainly due to the outcomes of interaction between the socialisee's inherent characteristics and the socialiser'; perspective on the goals for the socialisee. This latter approach to moulding and monitoring the nurtured's ideological behaviour is based on how the nurturant and the nurtured perceive the goals that should or could engender the behaviour of the child. Specifically the parenting styles are the outcomes of the different combinations of parental influence and child behaviour. The latter day psychologists have, therefore, moved to much wider definitions of parenting styles to include those which are democratic in communication and wider human thought. Democratic parenting style refers to the egalitarian interactive nature where the nurturer (meaning the parent) and the nurtured communicate, discuss, debate and arrive at compromises on the direction which the nurtured child should take. For example, a mother could direct a child towards disciplined behaviour. The child might debate the issue, might negotiate the reasons why he should behave in the direction indicated by the nurturer, and eventually the mother and child come to an acceptable compromise, where the mother offers an alternative and a satisfactory behaviour, different from the previous one. The child, therefore, compromises and agrees to behave the way indicated by the nurturant. For example, the mother might say to the child, "eat your dinner", the child may baulk, the mother might then offer an attraction and say if you eat your vegetables, then you can have a piece of chocolate which is the child's goal. This compromise is one situation where the child is brought around to perceive, to cognize and behave according to the indications of the mother's communication. This is the egalitarian approach for the situation where both the mother and the child agree to agree or agree to disagree on the basis of their own communicated needs.

The above personal determinants may occur singly or in conjunction with any or all. The term determinant as we have mentioned implies a characteristic that determines an individual's personality. What do we mean by personality? For this explanation we depend heavily upon three theories:

(1) Freudian theory or psychoanalytical theory,
(2) The social learning theory, and
(3) The theory of needs as explained by Allport (1954) and Maslow (1943).

It is pertinent to specify that any one of these major styles, namely, authoritarian, egalitarian or *laissez faire*, is constantly and consistently followed. Several times there may be abrupt breaks. For example, an exasperated or harassed mother who generally uses the *laissez faire* style might suddenly snap at the child and behave in an authoritarian manner, even if momentarily. Similar instances might occur with the other major predominant styles, and ideologies used in the parenting styles. Personalities do not consistently behave in the same way all the time. There may be other intervening factors which might cause abrupt breaks in the constant style and then reappear again dependent upon the reaction the child offers to the parenting stimulus. The same may be said of the other two major parenting styles in the ideologies in egalitarianism and *laissez faire*. Considering the dynamic patterns that act and react from one personality to another, such wavering patterns normally occur when personal and situational determinants keep changing. Besides the one-to-one interactive process where the predominant behaviour such as authoritarianism used by the parent as her normal style might suddenly come up with a barrier where the child instead of being submissive to the authoritarian parent could take a different stand. This is an impasse which the parent is confronted with and, therefore, at some time or the other, one of the two, the parent or the child, gives in. If we observe the dynamism of such confronting patterns, the will of the mother is pitted against the will of the child and in the face of who has the more power, the less powerful, in this case the child, usually gives in and conforms. Such breaks in the major patterning style occur some time, and also in the other two major styles, the egalitarian style and the *laissez faire* style. It is also not unusual that in any one episode there may be the use of more than one style at different rates of priority and strength depending upon the needs of either the parent or the child and the determinism and strength of the goal orientation. In many cases there may be trial and error in the style used. For example, the authoritarian parent might tend to be strict and regimented towards the child in the early years of childhood where the child is less experienced and the parent has a clearer idea about the direction towards which she would like the child to move towards. The attempt to fulfil needs may be strong in one and less so in the other. Similarly, the values of the adult may be stronger than the values of the child and therefore, parenting styles have an in-depth strength in them which the child weeds to by confront. However, as the child matures, gains experience and learns the pathways that the parent usually takes and has on his or her own part learned to resist and to offer alternatives which are predominantly the child's, in such cases of growing in maturity, of learning other alternatives due to the influence of peer groups or due to a higher need-fulfilment than that of the parent, the growing child usually moves away from dependency, which was a bonding format in the early years towards growing independency.

This two-way interaction is not without the influence of other factors both human as well as environmental. Other human factors which intervene are, for instance, the grandmother or the elderly relative rebuking the adult parent. Again, the authoritarian parent finding resistance in response to the direction, if in public might desists from controlling the child in order not to appear to be an unpleasant parent, but in private, the parent might scold or/and punish the child. At times, however, a parenting adult, for example, who is inclined to explain, discuss and persuade, in other words uses a democratic style, may find herself at a loss for explaining to or persuading the child and may become impatient and authoritarian, therefore, authoritative. What we are attempting to say is that though each one of these styles are the generally predominating ones, at times there is inconsistencies and perhaps the constancy of the styles breaks due to several other intervening variables, known and unknown. Such intervening variables are geo-ecological, socio-religious or ethnic in nature. This is but natural given the fact that behaviour is constantly affected by other factors, but the point still remains that more or less consistently and constantly the parenting adult behaves in one of the three major given styles with fluctuations occurring now and again.

From where does the authoritarian, egalitarian, democratic, casual or *laissez faire* types of behaviour accrue to a parenting adult? It is emphasized here that the parenting adult herself or himself is a product of their own socialisation used on them by their own parents. Since socialisation is a process, which leaves its mark on the socialized child, there is a tendency for imitation to occur. The parents during his or her own socialisation process imbibes the attitudes, the goals and the values as part of their own character which then they transfer on to their own children as a part of the evolutionary transference of characteristics. However, not all parents become authoritative or otherwise as do their parents. A parent, for instance, who has been strictly and heavily punished during her childhood, might consciously refrain from doing the same with her own child as she consciously feels the negativity has risen within her attitudes and behaviour which are similarly negative.

Added to this wavering parenting, where now and again the dominant style is inconsistent, are the other kinds of domination that overpower the parent herself. For example, the parent might be living in a joint family or in a family to which her mother-in-law has constant access and the latter may be frequently given to criticizing her daughter-in-law or daughter in their styles of raising the grandchildren. These interferences might then not only negate the major parenting style but also cause the parent to change to other styles in order to escape or avoid the influence of others on her style of upbringing of her children. Again, other intervening factors might be the economic factor of some times being able to afford what the child wants and some times not being able to afford such items as the child might constantly want and, therefore, brings about inconsistency in behaviour. This causes deviation in the major parenting style, indicating that every action brings about a reaction much depended upon the environmental stimuli, whether human or material. When we talk about a parenting style we mean a style which usually occurs in the interactive process between the parent and the child *per se*. In terms of social reality, however, the parent-child interaction is consciously or unconsciously influenced by other characteristics within the mother and similarly within the child. An authoritarian parent, for instance, might find at times complete compliance from the child because the child has been able to size up this situation, so to speak, and negotiates the overriding factors and chooses to comply only in order to gain an award, since the parenting adult is very authoritarian about that particular type of behaviour. For example, a primary school child knows that it is forbidden that he watches television before finishing his homework. He or she, therefore, tends to complete the homework really quickly in order to be able to watch his or her favourite show. In other words, the child is usually highly cued to the mother's behaviour and can plan ahead of the communication from his parent, who is rigid in her behaviour, finding devious ways of getting around the parent which appear innocent, but are frequently based on the child's perception of the known reactions of the parent. Thus, there is no such thing as normal behaviour, or abnormal behaviour. Behaviour is a conglomerate of different interactions which when taken together operationally stylize the parenting profile.

The Consequences of Parenting Action or Reaction

We have in the above sections, dealt upon parental attributes of the parenting adults and the consequences of parental interaction with the child. There is, however, the other side of the coin, namely child behavioural attributes. These are dynamic situations and changes in a dynamic manner even though it is a same adult and a same child. The child, however, is not a static figure. He has his own individualistic characteristics which, when interacting with the parent, can be resistant, acquiescent or indifferent. These tendencies emanate from his own personality and since no two personalities are alike, the interaction will differ from one parent-child to another parent-child. Parental behaviour is generally directed towards a goal/goals and usually is perceived in a long-term perspective. The question, from the parental point of view, is, "what I want my child to become?" The child's goals are usually short-term. His needs are such that there is need for quick fulfilment as and when a child pulls at his mother's hands, to say that "I want this", "I want that", without any relationship to the behavioural outcomes. As the child grows older, however, his maturity level increases with his experience. He encounters these experiences, either modulate his needs or heighten them simultaneously as he grows more mature and chronologically older. Social learning theory tells us that he learns to attune his needs not only to its fulfilment, but to its utility. He learns to temper down his needs to delay them to a further time. And, thus moves towards goal maturity. During this period of growing maturity, his personality also develops in such a way that he learns to attune his needs towards his personality attributes. The child is, therefore, a developing adult and like the adult he develops his own personality characteristics. We see this difference appearing in the child, who is in his primary school age of development, as compared with an adolescent. An adolescent will argue and not accept what his parent says/ wants to do. And in a way parents say "my child is learning to think for himself, he is not a baby I know". Thus, the older the child the more difficult the parenting success will be. The adolescent child tends to grow away from his parents and inherently tells itself: "I want to be what I want to be, I do not want to be moulded by my parents. I want to be an independent identity". The adolescent child, therefore, grows in independence in performing tasks and in decision-making. Confrontation with parent is much more apparent. Often the parent who has not been able to build up trust in relationships during the growing years find it difficult to control the adolescent child.

It is not to be assumed that there is a one-to-one relationship between the parenting style and its effect on the parented child. There are three aspects that interact to bring about the effect on the child thus parented. One is the parent herself who is more or less the constant caretaker from whom the child gains the influences. The parent may herself be of a certain type which may be indelibly of her making, having been parented herself when she herself was a child. It is usual, however, in most instances, that the parent is female and so engenders an environment of foisting certain influences which are of her own making, having been influenced by her own parent's personality and the atmosphere of her own childhood, whether in the home or an institution. For example, it is not unusual to hear relatives remark, "the granddaughter is so much like the grandmother". This may be true in most cases in reference to physiological, like the colour of the eyes, and psychological attributes. However, more often than not, the observant attributes are usually the mother's own personality making. She may turn out to be a miniature of her own mother, who herself may have been casually brought up, or is a mix of being authoritarian, and may most likely foist some of her authoritarian characteristic behaviour on her child. Again, this authoritarianism is a mix with the egalitarian or casual. behaviour. Often, however, one of the three or four parenting styles may be most predominant. It is not frequent that the mother is bereft of her own traits which she unconsciously influences the child to be moulded in her caretaking activities. At any given time, the most predominant style may be repeated so that it becomes the predominant feature in the parenting child. It is not unusual to hear comments like "the daughter behaves very much like her mother". It is, therefore, necessary to indicate that the rubric of behaviour while at times being autocratic or democratic or *laissez faire* more often than not is one ideological system. It is most unlikely, however, that females are more authoritarian because female children are more likely to imitate their mothers and since the mother has feminine attributes, the daughter is more likely to imitate her while the son is more likely to imitate the father, especially when the female caretaker says, shows a greater exhibition of behaving proudly of the father and saying, "I want you to grow-up to be a strong man like your father." That is why I am encouraging you to do well in sports and play cricket like your father does. On the other hand, if the mother influences the child to be more girlish, she will constantly tell her daughter not to be tomboyish and will encourage her to imitate feminine ways.

History tells us that the males are often authoritarian and females are more democratic, docile and submissive, which are probably an outcome of the mother's characteristics (Carson, Chowdhury, Perry and Pati, 1999).

Thus, it is obvious that the parenting style of the mother is quite predominant in the interaction, especially with the female child. If there is no male parent, the mother tends to uphold the most predominant male figure in the family and thereby uphold the patriarchal norms of the family.

In the holistic family circuit, the female caretaker acts and reacts with the child such that there is a pervasive stream of the generalized social class behaviour. If one were to examine the family for imitative models, then it becomes clear that social class characteristics like economic status, educational status and socio-religious beliefs are part of the general make-up of maternal influences. This happens on a normative basis. The mother tends to send her child to the same status school as do the families in the same socio-economic class. Further, her child may have a similar set of peer group, and cultural traits. As the child grows older, the child tends to adapt to the peer group norms rather than the norms of the parent group or to the adult behaviour in the family circuit much more than the behaviour of the rest of the family members.

The culture of the family also gradually tends to dominate the tendency of the parent to reinforce "monotropism" (Bowlby, 1952). In the lower class, however, the child tends to have multiple caretakers, since often the mother works outside the home to add to the family income. This tendency also infiltrates into the personality characteristics of the child through the mother's reinforcement. Frequently, the family tends to live close to other relatives of the family as perceived by those who live in *juggis* and *jhoparis* in the slum areas where the mother tends to leave the child during the day with female relatives who are not working, who look after groups of related children. In this context, grandmothers are very important figures for substitute caretaking. Thus, the child frequently tends to imbibe these patterns of caretaking that emanates from one related family member to another. In the urban areas, there is also the tendency to leave such young children to be looked after by day care centres run by the governments, municipalities and such like groups, which are often sponsored by a combination of Government and voluntary organizations (Khalakdina, 1998). In cases where there is no such help, the older siblings are kept away from schools, especially the adolescent females and this is part of the reason why female children drop out of school more often and earlier than the male children. The surrogate caretaker also takes care of the required household chores. If one looks at the scenario of heterogeneity in the eco sphere, another intervening variable, the ethic and the ethos, used by the family in particular ethnic groups, living in disparate regions such as the migrating Rajput families which migrate to cities *en masse* to regions which are more placable for the family to earn a stable income so as to provide for all members of the family. For instance, the utilisation of particular days for *pujas* and the distribution of *Prasad* which is an ethic shared by the family with its relatives closer by so as to maintain the ethics of devotion to particular godheads, where even relatives of the family, especially those who lives in proximity.

Each of the parenting styles appears to have certain influences on children's behaviour. However, culture also influences the outcome, especially for school success. The majority of parents fall into one of these categories most of the time. When parents are inconsistent in their parenting approach, it is very damaging to their children because they do not know what to expect.

Authoritarian Parenting

The use of punitive and forceful measures to enforce proper behaviour causes anger, resentment, and deceit and impairs wholesome parent-child relationships (Bettelheim, 1985). In Baumrind's 1967 research, preschoolers with authoritarian parents are withdrawn and unhappy. They appear anxious and insecure with peers and react hostilely if frustrated. Baumrind's 1971 research shows girls to be dependent and lacking in motivation and boys much more likely to be angry and defiant. In addition, children of authoritarian parents are less likely to internalize (accept as their own standard) society's unacceptable behaviours (Grusec and Goodnow, 1994) and are more likely to have low self-esteem (Coppersmith, 1967). These children often model their parents' inflexible thinking (Dekovic, Genis, and Janssens, 1992).

Baumrind described the three styles of parenting and the consequences of each of these styles on child's behaviour. However, when describing parental behaviour as to its effect on the child, it is necessary to remember that parental behaviour has to be consistent in one way or other of the three types. Wavering from one type to the other in parental interaction with the child, also finds inconsistent response from the child, where parents are inconsistent, the effect on the child is also inconsistent response so that any one type of parental behaviour does not bring in consistent child response.

Permissive Parenting

Parents who are non-punitive, loving, and accepting of the child often have children who lack independence and are selfish because they are not taught how their actions affect others. These children tend to be impulsive, aggressive, and low in taking responsibility.

Uninvolved or Permissive-Indifferent Parenting

The combination of permissiveness and indifference or rejection in varying degrees has detrimental effects on children. In the extreme, it becomes neglect, which is a form of child abuse (Stroufe, Egeland, Carlson and Collins, 2005). Children with few rules who are ignored or living with hostility are non-compliant and aggressive. They have low self-esteem and display anger towards others. Many exhibit anti-social behaviour and may end up as criminals (Straus, 1994; Brophy, 1992).

Authoritative Parenting

Parents who are nurturing and set, discuss, and enforce developmentally appropriate limits are the most successful in helping their children become autonomous, independent, self-controlled, self-confident, and cooperative (Grusec, Rudy and Martini, 1997; Baumrind, 1969; 1971). These children also are more likely to have high levels of competence and high self-esteem during middle childhood and adolescence (Coppersmith, 1967; Loeb, Horst, and Horton, 1980). They also have internalized moral standards (Holmbeck, Paikoff, and Brooks-Gunn, 1995) and their academic performance in high school is superior to that of children from either authoritarian or permissive homes (Dornbusch, Ritter, Leiderman, Roberts, and Fraleigh, 1987; Steinberg, Dornbush, and Brown, 1992).

In other words, democratic consistency bring about stability in the child's response to have high levels of competence and high self-esteem during middle childhood and adolescence.

6
Conclusion

It is essential at the end of this book that a round-up is presented of the ideas discussed in each of the chapters. So, this conclusion presents a round-up of the various ideologies of parenting styles in a synchronizing manner. For, it is to be remembered that there is a strong linkage between and among the ideas presented. The major parenting ideals have been derived from the three distinct ideologies. They are:

(1) Authoritarian parenting style in the upbringing or the caretaking phenomenon,
(2) Egalitarian style, and
(3) *Laissez faire* or casual style.

These three major types have been enunciated and analyzed. What probably is not clear from the available information on parenting styles is the lack of clear linkages among and between these three ideologies.

Therefore, an attempt has been made to unravel the salient factors that come into play in parents adopting different ideologies for parenting their children. These three major factors are:

(1) Personality factors,
(2) The situational circumstances, and
(3) A deeper insight into each one of the three ideologies.

The pattern of interaction between the nurturer and the nurtured is such that there is a syndrome of any one of patterns prevailing at any one time. The tightness of bondage or looseness of the bondage can occur at any time in a hypothetical manner as the features on which these patterns depend are innately joined together dependent upon the pattern of bonding between the nurturer and the nurtured. The two terms, the nurturer and the nurtured, have been used to indicate the giving and taking of the care. In this interactive pattern, there are many illustrations drawn to exemplify the phenomenon of giving and taking in the parent-child interaction. This is more especially true when it is noted that the interactive pattern is cohesive or disembodied or loosely joined so as to present the feature of change in the interaction. The pattern is also such that the cohesion of one with the other is dependent on the heaviness of the two interactors or the looseness. For the cohesion to happen it is essential to state the cognitive patterns changing from time-to-time. For instance, there have been many illustrations given of the different types of interactions in which one pattern of behaviour is stronger in one type than in another. The nurturer may desist from acting in cohesion with other interactors, or inter situations that may occur unexpectedly. Instead, the nurturer may be persistently retroactive or stubbornly resistant. This dependency or independency is again related to the personalities of the interactors, namely, the interactive parent or the interacted child. In other words, the pattern may vary according to the interactive patterns or the interacting personalities. At this point, it is essential to indicate that the nurturer and the nurtured who are in interactive process may from time-to-time behave in a disorderly fashion or unpredictable fashion where it is not possible to proactively specify the type of behaviour of either the nurturer or the nurtured.

For this reason, if not for any other, it is important to collate studies that deal with parenting practices and to devise methodologies to understand similarities or dissimilarities among parents interacting with the children.

There also needs to be a kind of a bibliography of studies which show similarity in the interactive patterns between the parent and child as also indicating where and how this happens in the various ethnic, regional, religious and socio-economic spheres. For example, studies that deal directly with the parent and the child in a given ecology, in a given religion, in a given ethnic group, would indicate cohesion in the parenting practices in the group studied. One can find similarities and differences in the correlative patterns in the interactive processes between the nurturer and the nurtured in there different settings. Thus, one might easily say, for instance, that socio-religious patterns of behaviour are similar among Gujaratis who practise one religion or among the people in a northern State. Such kind of cohesive pattern gradually evolves presenting to the readers similarities or dissimilarities as could be shown in the case, for instance, in the parenting practices of tribals in north India *vis-à-vis* tribals in south India.

The personality of parent or the child grows in strength as the individual grows in maturity, cognitively secure or insecure, and also growing in a cohesive collateral pattern, thus presenting to the reader various kinds of patterned behaviour.

These psycho-social trends can change from one minute to another, dependent also upon situational correlatives that interact with the giver or taker of the parenting style. For example, where there is a relatively loosely jointed interactive pattern the nurturant, if heavy-handed, will not give in to push or pull of the other patterns presented by either the nurturant or the nurtured. What is meant here is that it is not easy to identify a continuous conglomerate pattern of cohesiveness or non-cohesiveness and in fact the pattern might change from one situation to another where the nurturant is heavy-handed or loosely related to the nurtured. In other words, if there is heavy-handedness from the nurturer, this tendency tends to remain strong than in the given nurtured-nurturer behaviour. For example, if we examine the styles that have been highlighted by Super and Harkness, the latter tends to evoke similarities rather than dissimilarities in the patterned behaviour of the nurturer and the nurtured.

The very word authoritarian implies heavy-handedness used by the nurturant and loose disjointedness when used by the parent.

It is essential to state here that this pattern of interaction is held in collaboration with other factors like ecology, economy, climate and unforeseen factors which happen suddenly, but stay for a longer time, like for instance, climatic situations, like when there is an unexpected storm. It is also essential to state that the heavy handedness is usually controlled by the parent and is very often used to stabilize the pattern of behaviour of the nurturant. On the other hand, it is essential to state that the flippancy of movement from one pattern to another is also conducive to the light-handedness of the user of the technique, of one type or the other. For, there is always a light-handedness in being tolerant or heavy in interaction with the nurturant. The shifts in the system of movement from one pattern to another or from one ideology to another is strongly enforced by the interactiveness of the other factors which are heavy-handed such as the father being heavy-handed with the mother, who being authoritative tends to slip back into being lackadaisical or tends to become slow in response to the continuance of the style from time-to-time. As the child or the nurtured grows chronologically, he or she tends to decode the pattern of the nurturant and at time tends to pre-code the pattern that is used by the nurturer. This pre-coding behaviour in the nurtured is more prevalent with the authoritarian than with the egalitarian and, more so, with the *laissez faire* parent or the nurturer, as the steadiness of the use of a pattern tends to impose the style of the parenting nurturer. As the child grows chronologically, he or she tends to be more steadfast with the retaliative nature used when interacting with the parent. Thus, it is seen that the heaviness or light-handedness of the nurturer is an important standard status that is perceived by the nurtured as the years go by, for the nurturer tends to exhibit the pattern of behaviour constantly used as to confirm the fact that the nurturer is either authoritarian, *laissez faire* or egalitarian. Thus, it is observed that the pattern becomes discontinuous when changing of one ideology to another for the nurturer since there are three major styles tends to use one of the three more often than not, and not an amalgam of all three or any one of them. For, it is noticed that as the chronological age increases, the nurtured also tends to grow in one type of behaviour rather than the others. What is being said here is that in the interaction between the nurturer and the nurtured, there is very little choice as to which one will prevail the most, for it is obvious that it is either this or that style, as the parental figure tends to use only between two, if any, most of the time. If the nurturer is heavy-handed or highly authoritative, it is not possible to state that the parent is heavy-handed or not heavy-handed as the choice is only between the two. In other words, it is a uni-dimensional situation.

Thus what is being said here is that the nurturers might themselves interact in their interactive patterns from one time to another dependent upon their own childhood upbringing in their childhood. The nurturer might also tend to use the same pattern she or he has been accustomed in his or her upbringing when they were children. There may be interactive dissonance, for the nurturant may at times use her own upbringing pattern when she was a child or jump from one to another pattern, holding on to the pattern that was used on the parent in her childhood. In other words, the nurturant might himself or herself might focus on one or two styles and not use a myriad number of styles as some times happens when there is a joint family living situation.

Linearity

There are several activities which interact between the nurturer and the nurtured during the parenting process which require to be considered in understanding the outcome of such interactions.

Interactive Cohesion

When there is cohesive interaction, there is mutuality in the interactive process where the outcome is generally understood to be mutually of positive growth. For example, when the nurturant interacts with the nurtured, there is a tendency for positive growth to take place and for an understanding of each other's limitations and growth channels.

Changeability within the Ideology

The ideologies between the nurtured and the nurturer tend to change with the development of the growth from the nurturer to the nurtured. When there is cohesion between the two, the tendency is of the nurtured to be positively affected.

Continuity and Discontinuity

Further it is essential to state that continuity in the interaction process between the nurturer and nurtured form one of being cohesive to being discontinuous. This happens in the process of interaction between the nurturer and the nurtured. In other words, there is no linearity that can be identified from the nurturer to the nurtured. In these differing processes, there might be clashes between and among the same sex child and the differently approachable manner in which the nurturance takes place. When it is the situation of the one sex child in the family, then there is congeniality in the process of nurturance. But when there are more than one sex in the children who are being reared, there is the question how to deal with the difference in sex when the interaction is differently posed by the nurturant with one sex in comparison to the other sex in the family of many children.

Sex and Congeniality

In the upbringing process, it is necessary to realize that there is the distinction that is to be made between the sexes, namely the mother upbringing the male child as well as the female child.

Thus, it should be considered that not only is there a gender factor between the nurturer and the nurtured, but these gender factors operate at the same time in the process of nurturance. The mother, for instance, might view the development of the girl child differently from the way she views the development of the male child. In the process of nurture, there are many differentially impinging factors, dependent upon whether the family has to deal with one sex child or many sex children which might give rise to tendencies in the way the ideology is implemented. Therefore, what is being said here is that differences in sexes in one family might give rise to differential nurturing process. As such the process of nurturance will differ from one particular family to another. In this way, the experiences of the nurtured child in one family situation will be different from another family situation, given the variety of actors that operate in one family *versus* another. Therefore, it is essential to consider the upbringing process as being differentially experienced from one family to another.

It is essential also to consider the fact that each nurturer brings to the nurturing process her own childhood experiences which will affect the nurturing procedure the nurturer uses in bringing up similar sexed child and children of different sexes, and further still multi-factored children, i.e. differentiated not only on the basis of gender but also other factors such as age.

Essentially, therefore, the nurturing procedure is influenced by many factors and each factor, namely age, sex, and the differential ideologies the parent brings to the nurturance, and the action and reaction between the nurturer and the nurtured, will change over time and space.

Bibliography

Abdul Kalam, APJ and Sujan Pal Singh, (2011), *Innovative Solutions towards Sustainable Development*. Delhi: Penguin Publishers.

Allport, G.W. (1954), *The Nature of Prejudice*. Cambridge: M.A. Addison-Wesley.

Atkinson, J.W. (ed.) (1958), *Motives in Fantasy, Action and Society*. Princeton N.J.: Van Nostrand.

Bagley, C., Iwawaki, S. and Young, L. (1983), "Japanese Children: Group Oriented but not Field-dependent", in C. Bagley and G. Verma (eds.), *Multi-cultural Childhood*. Aldershot: Gower, pp. 27-317.

Bandura, A. (1977), *Social Learning Theory*. Englewood Cliffs, N.J.: Prentice Hall.

Baum, D. (2008), "Reading a phylogenetic tree: The meaning of monophyletic group", *Nature Education* 1(1) Wisconsin, USA.

Baumrind, D. (1966), "Effects of Authoritative Parental Control on Child Behaviour", *Child Development*, 37(4): 887-907.

Baumrind, D. (1971), "Current Patterns of Parental Authority", *Developmental Psychology (Monographs)*, 4 (1): Pt. 2.

Baumrind, D. (1991), "Parenting styles and adolescent development", in J. Brooks-Gunn, R. Lemer, and A.G. Petersen (eds.), *The Encyclopaedia of Adolescence*. New York: Garland.

Bettelheim, Bruno (1985), *A Home for the Heart*. Chicago: University of Chicago Press (originally published in 1974).

Bhat, P.N. Mari and Shiva S. Halli (1999), "Demography of Bride-price and Dowry: Causes and Consequences of the Indian Marriage Squeeze." *Population Studies*, 53 (2): 129-148.

Biggs, J.B. (1992), "Learning and Schooling in Ethnic Chinese: An Asian Solution to a Western Problem", in S. Lau (ed.), *Growing UP: The Chinese Way: Chinese Child and Adolescent Development*, Hong Kong: Chinese University Press, 147-167.

Bowlby, J. (1952), "Maternal Care and Mental Health", *Journal of Consulting Psychology*, 16(3): 232.

Bright, W. (2000), *Cultural Anthropology Today*. Dehmar. California: CRM Books.

Brody, Leslie (1999), *Gender, Emotion and the Family.* Combridge, M.A.: Harward University Press.

Bronfenbrenner, U. (1970), *Two Worlds of Childhood: U.S. and USSR.* London: Russel Sage.

Bronfenbrenner, U. (1979), *The Ecology of Human Development*. Cambridge, M.A.: Harvard University Press.

Brophy, J. (1992), "Probing the subtleties of subject-matter teaching", *Educational Leadership*, 49(7): 4-8.

Buri, J.R. (1989), "Self-esteem and Appraisals of Parental Behaviour", *Journal of Adolescent Research*, 4: 33-49.

Burkitt, I. (1992), *Social Selves: Theories of the Social Formation of Personality*, London: Sage Publications.

Carson, D.K., Chowdhury A., Perry C.K., and Patic, C. (1999), "Family Characteristics and Adolescent Competence in India: Investigation of Youth in Southern Orissa", *Journal of Young and Adolescence*, 28(2). Chaudhry, Minakshi (1998), *Exploring Pangi Himalaya: A World Beyond Civilization*, Delhi: Indus Publishing.

Cline, Foster and Jim Fay (2006), *Parenting with Love and Logic: Teaching Children Responsibility*. Colorado Springs: Pinion Press.

Coppersmith, S. (1967), *The Antecedents of Self-esteem*. San Francisco: W.H. Freeman & Co.

Darling, Nancy, (1999) "Parenting Style and its Correlates", *Eric Digest*, March.

Darling, Nancy and Lawrence Steinberg (1993), "Parenting Styles as Context: An Integrative Model", *Psychological Bulletin*, 113 (3): 487-496.

Deater-Deckard, K. and Dodge, K.A. (1997) "Externalizing behaviour problems and discipline revisited: Non-linear effects and variation by culture, context and gender", *Psychological Inquiry*, Vol. 8, pp. 161-75.

Deater-Deckard, K., Lansford, J., Dodge, K., Pettit, G., and Bates, J. (2003), "The development of attitudes about physical punishment: An 8-year longitudinal study", *Journal of Family Psychology*, 17 (3).

Dekoviç, M., and Janssens, J.M.A.M. (1992), "Parents' Child-rearing Style and Child's Sociometric Status", *Developmental Psychology*, 28: 925-932.

Dornbusch, S.M., Ritter, P.L., Liederman, P., Roberts, D., and Fraleigh, M. (1987). "The Relation of Parenting Style to Adolescent School Performance", *Child Development*, 58: 1244-1257.

Doshi, S. (ed.), (1971), *Bhils: Between Societal Self-Awareness and Cultural Synthesis*. New Delhi: Sterling Publishers.

Erikson, E.H. (1968), *Identity, Youth, and Crisis*. New York: MacMillan.

Erickson, E.H. (1977), *Childhood and Society*, St. Albans: Triad/Paladin.

Eysenck, H.J. (1990), "Genetic and environmental contributions to individual differences: The three major dimensions of personality", *Journal of Personality, 58*: 245-261.

Freud, S, (1935), *General Introduction to Psycho Analysis*, New York: Liveright.

Freud, A., (1946), *The Ego and Mechanisms of Defence*, New York: International University Press.

Freud, S. (1953) [Originally published in 1890], *The Interpretation of Dreams*. Volumes 4-5 of *the Standard Edition of the Complete Psychological Works of Sigmund Freud*. London: Hogarth; New York: MacMillan.

Fuller, J.L. (1960), "Behaviour Genetics", *Annual Review of Psychology*. 11: 41-70.

Gottlieb, G. (2003), "Probabilistic Epigenesis of Development", in J. Valsiner and K.J. Connolly (Eds.), *Handbook of Developmental Psychology*, London: Sage, 3-17.

Grusec, J.E., and Goodnow, J.J. (1994), "Impact of Parental Discipline Methods on the Child's Internalization of Values: A Reconceptualization of Current Points of View", *Developmental Psychology*, 30: 4-19.

Grusec, J.E., Rudy, D., and Martini, T. (1997) "Parenting cognitions and child outcomes: an overview and implications for children's internalization of values." In J.E. Grusec and L. Kuczynski (Eds.), *Parenting and Children's Internalization of Values: A Handbook of Contemporary Theory*. New York: Wiley, pp. 259-282.

Hall, Calvin S., Gardner Lindzey and John B. Campbell (eds.) (1998), *Theories of Personality*, John Wiley & Sons Inc., New York.

Haviland, A., (2002), *Cultural Anthropology*. 10th edition. USA: Harcourt Collage Publishers.

Hoff, E., Laursen, B. and Tardif, T. (2002) "Socio-economic Status and Parenting", in M.H. Bornstein (ed.), *Handbook of Parenting*. Volume 2: *Biology and Ecology of Parenting* (2nd edition). Mahwah, NJ: Lawrence Erlbaum Associates.

Holden, George (1989), "Parental Attitudes Towards Child Rearing: Instruments, Issues and Implications", *Psychological Bulletin*, 106 (1): 29-58.

Holden, G.W., and Buck, J.M. (2002), *Parents and the Dynamics of Child-rearing*. Boulder. CO: Westview.

Holmbeck, G.N., Paikoff, R.L., and Brooks-Gunn, J. (1995), "Parenting Adolescents", in M. Bornstein (ed.), *Handbook of Parenting*: Vol. 1. *Children and Parenting* (pp. 91-118). Mahwah, NJ: Erlbaum.

Jodhka, Surinder S. (2001), *Community and Identities: Contemporary Discourses on Culture and Politics in India*. New Delhi: Sage Publications.

Jung, C.G. (1961), *The Theory of Psycho-analysis. A Collected Works*. Princeton: Princeton University Press.

Kakar, Sudhir (2012), *The Inner World: A Psychoanalytic Study of Childhood and Society in India*, Delhi: Oxford University Press.

Kaur, Ravinder (2001), "The Eclipse or the Renaissance of 'Community'? The Career of the Concept", in Surinder S. Jodhka (2001), *Community and Identities: Contemporary Discourses on Culture and Politics in India*. New Delhi: Sage Publications, pp. 80-94.

Khalakdina, M. (1998), *"Early Childhood Care and Education in India"*, in M. Swaminathan (ed.), *First Five Years*, New Delhi: Sage Publications, pp. 163-194.

Khalakdina, M. (1998), "In Sight—On Site: Day Care for Construction Workers' Children", in M. Swaminathan (ed.), *First Five Years*, New Delhi: Sage Publications, pp. 44-59.

Khalakdina, M. (2011), *Human Development in the Indian Context: A Socio-cultural Focus*, Vol. 2. New Delhi: Sage Publications.

Khalakinda, M. (2012), *The Development of Personality in the Indian Ecology*, Chapter 3: "Theoretical Bases of Personality Development", pp. 113-142, New Delhi: Concept Publishing Company Pvt. Ltd.

Kohlberg, Lawrence (1976), "Moral stages and Moralisation: The cognitive developmental approach", in Thomas Lickona (ed.), *Moral Development and Behaviour: Theory, Research and Social Issues*. New York: Holt, Rinehart and Winston.

Krech, David and George S. Klein (1952), *Theoretical Models and Personality Theory*. Durham: Duke University Press, pp. 90-92.

Lamborn, S.D., Mounts, N.S., Steinberg, L. and Dornbusch, S.M. (1991), "Authoritative parenting and adolescent adjustment across varied ecological niches", *Journal of Research on Adolescence*, 1: 19-36.

Levine, Nancy E. (2008), "Alternative Kinship, Marriage, and Reproduction", *Annual Review of Anthropology*, Vol. 37: 375-389, October.

Lewin, K. (1935), *A Dynamic Theory of Personality*. New York: McGraw-Hill.

Lewin, K. (1936), *Principles of Topological Psychology*. New York: McGraw Hill.

Lewin, K. (1951), *Field Theory in Social Science: Selected Theoretical Papers*. New York: Harper & Row.

Lewin, K., Lippit, R., and White, (1939), "Patterns of Aggressive Behaviour in Experimentally Created Social Climates", *Journal of Social Psychology*, 10: 271-279.

Linda, S. Budd (1993), *Living with the Active Alert Child: Ground-breaking Strategies for Parents*, Seattle, Washington: Parenting Press.

Lippitt, R. (1964), "An Experimental study of Authoritarian and Democratic Group Atmospheres", in *Studies in Topological and Vector Psychology*, University of Lowa Studies in Child Welfare, No. 16.

Maccoby, E.E. and Martin, J.A. (1983), "Socialization in the context of the family: Parent-Child interaction", In P.H. Mussen and E.M. Hetherington, *Handbook of Child Psychology:* Vol. 4. *Socialization, Personality, and Social Development* (4th ed.). New York: Wiley.

Maslow, A.H. (1943), "The Theory of Human Motivation", *Psychological Review,* 50: 370-396.

Maslow, A.H. (1948), "Some Theoretical Consequence of Basic Need Gratification", *Journal of Personality,* 16: 402-416.

Maslow, A.H. (1970), *Motivation and Personality.* New York: Harper & Row.

McClelland, D.C. (1961), *The Achieving Society.* Free Press, New York.

Miller, N.E. (1944), "Experimental Studies of Conflict", in J.M. Hunt (ed.), *Personality and the Behaviour Disorders,* Vol. 1, New York: Ronald.

Miller, N.E., (1948), "Theory and Experiment Relating Psycho-analytic Displacement to Stimulus-Response Generalization", *Journal of Abnormal and Social Psychology,* 43: 155-178.

Miller, N.E. (1959), "Liberalization of Basic S-R Concepts: Extension to Conflict Behaviour, Motivation, and Social Learning", in S. Koch (ed.), *Psychology: A Study of Science* (Vol. 2). New York: McGraw Hill.

Moorhead, Joanna (2015), "When Does Laissez-faire Parenting Become Neglect", *The Independent,* 5 February, 2015.

Murray, H.A. (1938), *Explorations in Personality.* New York: Oxford University Press.

James Owen (2009), "Future Humans: Four Ways We May, or May Not, Evolve", *National Geographic News,* November 24, 2009. Web Source: URL: http://news.nationalgeographic.com/news/2009/11/091124-origin-of-species-150-darwin-human-evolution.html.

Parsons, T. (1967), *Sociological Theory and Modern Society,* New York: Free Press.

Penfield, W. and T. Rasmussen (1950), *The Cerebral Cortex of Man.* New York: MacMillan.

Piaget J., (1929), *The Child's Conception of the World.* London: Routledge and Kegan Paul.

Piaget, J., and B. Inhelder (1969), *The Psychology of the Child.* New York: Basic Books.

Phoenix, A., and F. Husain (2007), *Parenting and Ethnicity.* London, UK: Joseph Rowntree Foundation.

Ridley, M. (2006), *Genome.* New York: Harper Perennial.

Sanagavarapu, Prathyusha (2010), "What Does Cultural Globalisation Mean for Parenting in Immigrant Families in the 21st Century?", *Australasian Journal of Early Childhood,* 35 (2), June.

Saraswati, T.S. (ed.) (1999), *Culture, Socialisation and Human Development.* New Delhi: Sage Publications.

Shweder, Richard A.; Haidt Jonathan; Randall Horton and Craig Joseph (2008), "The Cultural Psychology of the Emotions: Ancient and

Renewed", in Michael Lewis *et al.* (eds.), *Handbook of Emotions*, 3rd edition, New York: The Guilford Press, pp. 409-427.

Sears, R.R., (1951), "Social Behaviour and Personality Development", in T. Parsons and E.A. Shills (eds.), *Toward a General Theory of Action*. Cambridge, Mass: Harvard University Press, 465-478.

Sears, R.R.; Maccoby, Eleanor E., and Levin, H. (1957) *Patterns of Child Rearing*. Evanston, 111, Row, Peterson.

Skinner, B.F. (1938). *The Behaviour of Organisms: An Experimental Analysis*. New York: Appleton-Century.

Skinner, B.F. (1948), "Superstition in the Pigeon", *Journal of Experimental Psychology*, 38: 168-172.

Skinner, B.F. (1974), *About Behavourism*. New York: Knopf.

Smelter, N. (1969), *Mechanism of Change and Adjustment of Change*, Germany: Rinehart and Winston Ltd.

Sroufe, A., Egeland, B., Carlson, E. and Collins, W. (2005), The *Development of the Person: The Minnesota Study of Risk and Adaptation from Birth to Adulthood*, New York: The Guildford Press.

Steinberg, L., Dornbush, S.M. and Brown, (1992), "Ethnic differences in adolescent achievement. An ecological perspective", *American Psychologist*, June, 47(6): 723-729.

Steinberg, L., Lamborn, S., Darling, N., Mounts, N., and Dornbusch, S.M. (1994), "Over-time changes in adjustment and competence among adolescents from authoritative, authoritarian, indulgent, and neglectful families", *Child Development*, 65: 754-770.

Straus, Murray A. (1994), *Beating the Devil Out of Them: Corporal Punishment in American Families*, San Francisco: CA: Jossey-Bass/ Lexington.

Super, S. and Harkness, "The Developmental Niche: A Conceptualisation on the Interface of Child and Culture", *International Journal of Behavioural Development*, 9: 545-69.

Watson, J.B. (1913), "Psychology as the Behaviourists View It", *Psychological Review*, 20: 158-178.

Werner, H. (1957), "The Concept of Development from a Comparative and Orgaismic Point of View", in D. Harris (Ed.), *The Concept of Development*. Minneapolis, Minnesota: University of Minnesota Press.

Woodhead, Martin (1987), "The Needs of Children: Is there Any Value in the Concept?", *Oxford Review of Education*, 13 (2): 129-139.

Index